Plate 168: The man second from the Barkway, man in middle of front ro action in 1918 in France.

Plate 178: The Evangelists were known as the 'Alexander Tory' well known for their 'Count your Many Blessings'.

Plate 205: Line 3 should read Edie Hawes not Eddie.

Plate 207: Back row should read from left to right: B. Clarke, A. Hawes, H. Casburn, W. Casburn & C. Stewart.

Plate 209: Vivienne should read Eileen and Eileen should read Vivienne.

Two stories are told by Mr Harry Davey, the first concerning Mr McBeath. Mrs Grainger asked Harry when he was a schoolboy to take her elderly cat and dog to Mr McBeath to have them put to sleep. Mr McBeath put the animals in a tea chest and asked Harry to sit on the lid whilst he mixed the potion. The first mixture was not strong enough so a stronger one was mixed whilst Harry still sat on top of the tea chest.

The other story concerns a Mr Charles Symons who died in 1915 and lived behind Inglenooks. He used to have a copper boiling pan which was let out for the villagers to make their brews. A boat oar was used to mix the potions which was then taken home by wheelbarrow. It seems the business closed when Customs and Excise moved in.

Firstly I would like to apologises to Mrs Houghton whose name is misspelt under plates 7, 17, 22, 38, 40-2, 45, 84-5, 92, 97, 199 & 204, and to the owners of house number 35 North Street where the date of their house on Page 145 6th line 1857, should read 1587.

Front cover photograph: the first boy on the right is Geof Campbell, the one behind is Don Fletcher and the one behind him Mrs Symons. Behind Mrs Symons is Stephen Llewellyn Albine Hunt (known as Albine). He was born Jerusalem in 1895 and was grandson of the Hunt mentioned in the Burwell Alphabet of 1862. The policeman is Albert Bonnet dressed up as a policeman while the couple on the left are Mr & Mrs King.

Plate 11: Second row should read Mag instead of May.

Plate 13: Gentleman on the far left is Cecil Brown

Plate 27: The little boy in the cap is Jim Fletcher.

Plate 58: Middle row, sixth from left is Mrs M. Rose's grandmother. The little boy sitting in front of Mrs Ridgeon is her son.

Plate 76: is actually the British Infant School and not St. Marys.

Plate 80: ?? Should be Anthony Frost and Jacqueline Heron.

Plate 121: The man in the middle is Herbert Warren and the man on the right Samie Attmore.

Plate 136: Should read Dr Ennion's children not Dr Elliott's.

Plate 138: The man in the middle of the door back row is Mr Fletcher Holder of the DCM from the first world war.

Plate 139: The man sitting on the grass near the dog is Mr G. Fuller.

Plate 154: The boy fourth from right front row is Derek Oliver.

BURWELL

A STROLL THROUGH HISTORY

Heather M. Richardson

Copyright © 1990
Published by H.M. Richardson Publishing
51 Garden Walk, Cambridge CB4 3EW
Printed in England by Black Bear Press,
King's Hedges Road, Cambridge CB4 2PQ

Cover illustration: Church parade led by Bombadier Fuller
and the Burwell Band. (G)
Title page illustration: Burwell crest taken from a piece
of Carlton china, marked: 'agent, Mark Chapman'.
Courtesy Mr Alan Brampton

ISBN 0 9516592 0 0

*I dedicate this book to
Eleanor, Patsy, Sheila, and Elizabeth,
and to the Glory of God,
through whom all things are possible.*

Foreward

To read Heather Richardson's *Stroll Through Burwell* has been both a privilege and a real delight. She has written with infectious enthusiasm and painstaking devotion to bring the past to life. That past is not only her own, not even that only of those of us who know and love and would preserve Burwell, but it is the history of all who recognise in Heather's pages characters who are as familiar and as close as the soil and the institutions which nourished and nurtured them.

We must thank Heather for the many hours of intensive research which she has undertaken. If her book pleases its readers, of whom I am sure there will be many, as much as it has done me, if it captures their imaginations and inspires them to look and to find, to cherish and keep, then the time spent on its production will have been of the greatest worth.

Violet M. Hills
Burwell,

October 1990

Acknowledgements

It never crossed my mind when I visited the reference library in the Lion Yard in February 1989 to view Mrs Grainger's photographs, that I would write a book about Burwell, but it was obvious after two or three visits to the library that the photographs had created a great deal of interest for many people. Reflecting on this I realised that before his death Mr Albert Gathercole had given me copies of his articles on the history of Burwell which he had written for Clunch magazine. Having never written a book, or anything else for that matter, I was very apprehensive about starting on such a venture and wondered why no-one had already attempted to write a book specifically about Burwell. The more I thought about it the more the idea appealed to me and so I ventured into the Cambridgeshire Collection of the City Library to see what else might be of interest there. It was quite amazing and exciting if one took the trouble to search for it.

This book would not have been at all possible without Mike Petty and his staff at the Cambridgeshire collection in the City Library, who so willingly helped me in my research and I am very grateful to them for their patience and the help they so willingly gave, including the copying and giving permission to use many of their photographs. I am also indebted to the staff of the County Records Office at the Shire Hall for information and photographs; the editors of the Cambridge Evening News and the Newmarket Journal for permission to use material from some of their articles; the Cambridge Antiquarian Society for permission to use some of their photographs; the Harrap Publishing Group Ltd for permission to use information from J. Wentworth Day's book, History of the Fens; Mr Jim Townsend for giving me the opportunity to see and photograph the 1842 tithe map; Mr Jim Neale for permission to use material from his book, Illustrated History of the Burwell and District Motor Service, and for allowing me to use some of his photographs; to Mr Alan Bampton for providing me with a photograph of the piece of china with the Burwell crest; my thanks are also due to Dr Bruce Winter, the Warden of Tyndale House for permission to use its facilities to produce camera ready copy. Other people who have kindly lent photographs, newscuttings or who have helped in other ways, include, the Cambridge and Burwell Branch of the British Red Cross Society, Mrs Olive Johnson, Miss Winifred Peachey, Mrs F. Houghton, Mr and Mrs E. Jacobs, Mr Ernie Palmer, Mr John Spence, Editor of Clunch and all those who got in touch with me following an article about the forthcoming book in the Newmarket Journal; to the Vicar of St. Mary's Church the Revd. I. Secrett for allowing my husband to take photographs inside the Church; to Mrs Kate Hills, Miss Violet Hills, Miss Brenda Carter, and my mother, Mrs Mabel R. Johnson for reading through the manuscript and giving me helpful advice, and to my husband John, and Jane Langley for proof reading and editing the text.

Lastly but not least I wish to thank my son Tony for helpful advice on layout, designing and producing the cover at Norman Harding Design and Print, and for preparing the photographs for publication.

The photographs, unless otherwise stated are from the Cambridgeshire Collection but for the interest of readers I have marked those from the Grainger collection with (G).

I make no apologies for the large part of the text devoted to the churches and chapels. Life, in days gone by, was lived around its religious buildings and made up much of its history. Despite the odd murder and other misdemeanours I believe, like our country, that Burwell was a Christian village as much of the information reveals. Every effort has been made to ensure the facts throughout the book are correct. However I quite think there is much more to tell, and as more information comes to hand there is no reason why at some time in the future, the material within these pages could not be updated, and photographs identified and added to.

Heather M. Richardson
Cambridge

October 1990

BURWELL ALPHABET OF 1862 by G.H. Clifton

A   Was an Anderson lazy and slow.
B   Was Tom Ball and Richard the Co.
C   Were the Casburns of whom there are flocks.
D   Was a Danby that lived at the Fox.
E   Was Miss Eastwell whom Martin did charm her.
F   Was a Fuller who once was a farmer.
G   Was a Gardiner, a builder not quick.
H   Was a Hunt, a layer of brick.
I   Was an innkeeper, John Carter they called.
J   Was Tom Johnson of Tunbridge and Hall.
K   Was Joe Kent who of draughts took enough.
L   Was a Lucas, a taker of snuff.
M   Was a Mingay whose bus was his life.
N   Was Jack Nickols chastising his wife.
O   Was an Oliver, a grinder of flour.
P   Was John Peachey, right High Chancellor.
Q   Was a query if Fielder was right.
R   Was a Roddicar joyous and bright.
S   Was a Stays an artist self-made.
T   Was a Turner by name and by trade.
U   Was an Umpire who never was wrong.
V   Was a Vicar both hearty and strong.
W   Was Sweet William, whose surname was Dunn.
X   The expense attending his fund.
Y   Were the Youths of Burwell far-famed.
Z   We leave for want of a name.

THE KEY TO THE BURWELL ALPHABET by Charles Lucas

A   *Isaac Anderson* was one of the cricket team, a good bat, but a slacker at fielding.

B   *Mr T.T. Ball*, a chemical manure manufacturer, who had recently taken his brother Richard into partnership, and was known by his intimates as 'The Co'.

C   *The families of the Casburns* were then very numerous in the village.

D   *William Danby*, a very respectable and good old tradesman kept the Fox Inn, which was considered one of the best conducted inns in the village, at which house most of the meetings, public dinners, and sales were held.

E   *Miss Eastwell*, whose personal appearance, manners, and conversation were greatly admired by a Mr William Martin, a carpenter.

F   *William Fuller*, who sold his land and farm to my father, and lived upright afterwards at Cambridge (as the people about here say).

G   *Mr Gardiner*, a good builder and contractor, but some thought perhaps he might have been a little quicker in completing his work.

H   *John Hunt*, a master-craftsman in the art of laying bricks.

I   *John Carter*, brewer, maltster, and proprietor of the White Horse Inn, was considered a good judge of horseflesh, and was known far and wide by dealers and others who came and stayed at his house for Reach Fair.

J   *Mr Thomas Johnson*, who lived at the Hall was a frequent visitor at the 'Tunbridge' and was thought by some folks to be a representative of both houses.

K   *Joe Kent* was a wealthy farmer of Swaffham Prior and suffered from nerves; he liked to see his medical attendant every morning, and took four draughts daily.

L   *Thomas Lucas*, who lived in the snuff-taking age. His well-known box with polished Scotch pebble lid, in silver setting, was produced on all occasions for folks to take a friendly pinch. Then the 'gravel path' was often seen on the lapels of his frock-coat.

M   *Henry Mingay* was a thrifty yeoman farmer who had a carrier's cart and drove a bus, called 'Perseverance'. He had a cheery smile and friendly joke for all his passengers.

N   *Jack Nichols*, a pork butcher, loved strong ale, and when he had been to an inn, and taken more ale than was good for him, would return home and chastise his wife, and her loud protestations often alarmed the neighbours.

O   *Oliver Carter* was a stout old miller who wore a white hat, and brought grist to his mill in a yellow cart with red shafts and wheels.

P   *John Peachy*, a boggling, big old man, who once appeared (with others) at a London law court on a charge of not paying his lawful dues on his Fenland. The knowledge of lawyers and law he acquired there was vast, and when he was 'fresh' his gesticulations were so violent that the folks in North Street conferred on him the title of 'Lord Chancellor'.

Q   *Mr Fielder*, a graduate of Jesus College, Cambridge, used to spend months together at Five Miles from Anywhere Inn, Upware, and from the frequenters of that inn formed a Republic and constituted himself President. But his satirical remarks on some of the Fen magnates made them question if the man was in his right mind.

R   (*Roddicar*) *Mr Robert Peachey* was a bustling old stock-jobber with a beaming countenance, happy smile, and cheery word; did everything with a swing.

S   (*Stays*) *William Peachey*, the village fop, who was reputed to have worn stays to preserve the symmetry of his figure. He was infatuated with a lady and used to paint her portrait and put it in her summerhouse.

T   *William Turner*, a clever manipulator of wood, a great protégé of my father, who liked to chat with him when at work. The old carpenter would often remark, 'I never go to church when there is a gathering. I don't hold with the University taking sixteen hundred pounds a year out of the parish without paying all dues and demands'.

U   *Bill Dunn*, whose knowledge of cricket was very limited, never would allow that he gave a wrong ruling in the game.

V   *The Rev J.W. Cockshott*, the vicar, was a man of stupendous energy and great endurance. The church he restored, the schools he built, and the good works he did in the parish in getting the young men and women good situations in life, and keeping in touch with them afterwards, will ever be remembered in the Burwell annals.

W   *Mr William Dunn*, whose brown, rubicund, and gnarled countenance suggested the flower sweet-william going off blossom.

X   *Mr Dunn* was the treasurer of the Cricket Club, and his own expenses in collecting the subscriptions had to be considered.

Y   *The Youths of Burwell far famed* improved 'the shining hours' by making harmless fun of the Burwell celebrities.

Z   No one in the village answered to this name.

The village of Burwell lies about twelve miles North-East of Cambridge, four miles North-West of Newmarket, about twelve miles South-East of Ely and sixty-five miles from London. It is the second largest village in Cambridgeshire and stretches about seven miles from north to south and about four miles from east to west, which is probably why it is sometimes referred to as Long Burwell Another Burwell exists in this country, in Lincolnshire. Moreover, a Port Burwell, a holiday resort, stands beside the beautiful Lake Erie in Ontario. The village in Cambridgeshire has a history probably going back nearly three thousand years and it is very likely that it started as a number of small settlements. In 1060 it's name was spelt Burewell but later spellings include Burewells, Borewelle, Burweile, Burella, Buruella, Buruuella, Burwelle, the latter two appearing in the Domesday Book. The present spelling which did not remain constant until the seventeenth century occurred for the first time in 1227, the year of the plague, from which the village suffered badly. The spelling of Burwells, which was also used, probably shows that the village was later in two parts, 'High Town', which was the earliest part, and 'Low Town', the name, which is a derivation of wielle and burg, meaning 'spring by the fort'.

Along the B1102 Swaffham Road, the Devil's Dyke marks the boundary between Swaffham Prior and Burwell. Old maps refer to it as the Great Ditch but survey maps call it Devil's Ditch. It is probably the longest dyke in the country, running in almost a straight line for seven and a half miles, beginning at the village of Reach and ending at the village of Wood Ditton. It is built up of layers of clunch and chalk, being some fifteen feet high in places. The ditches which run alongside, and from which the earth was taken, are twelve feet deep. Many theories have been put forward as to why it was constructed, one being that the devil himself built it in one night. It seems much more likely that it was built by the Anglo Saxons over a thousand years ago as a military defence. It has been suggested that it would have taken five hundred men working for three years, or fifty men for thirty years, each quarrying and redepositing two tons of chalk a day to construct it, and that thirteen thousand men standing in a straight line would have been needed to man it. A coin, dated 350 AD was found at one time below the old land surface and several excavations have been made over the years. In 1894, a man by the name of Atkinson discovered the foundations of a Roman house near the old Mildenhall to Cambridge railway line, and nearby, Sir Cyril Fox unearthed some remnants of Roman pottery. Just beyond here is the highest point known as Galley Hill and tradition has it that a Joe Badcock was hanged and gibbetted here for murdering his sweetheart. It was in the direct line of vision of the cottage door of the victim's parents at Reach so that they could see the 'fowls of the air fly away with pieces of flesh picked from his body'. In 1973, Dr Brian Hope Taylor, an eminent archaeologist, whilst excavating prior to the building of the Newmarket by-pass found a male skeleton. The skeleton's right hand was missing and it was thought that he was either buried during the construction of the dyke or shortly after. Perhaps he was caught stealing as for an offence of this nature, it was common practice to cut off the hand as a punishment.

Plate 1. Devil's Ditch, about 1930.

Originally the dyke was only breached in one place but when Dr Charles Lucas wrote his book, The Fenman's World published in 1930, he stated that there were five roads, two railways, and five assorted tracks and paths through the dyke. Now of course there is the Newmarket by-pass. Sheep and rabbits once grazed along the dyke and kept back the hedges and the undergrowth and when I walked its pathways during the 1950s it was possible to squeeze through, although I never actually walked the whole length in one go. On one of my jaunts towards Newmarket heath, I had rather an unpleasant encounter. Having walked about a quarter of a mile to a small clearing I came upon a vast number of rabbits, of all shapes, sizes and colours. They were staring at me in the most unnatural manner, with bulging eyes and swollen bodies. They seemed to leap about and did not bother to run away on seeing me, which was quite uncanny, very frightening and distressing. These rabbits had been subjected to a fatal disease caused by a virus, namely myxomatosis, which was used to keep down their population. Scrambling down the bank, more emerged from the undergrowth and I ran across the ploughed field away from the dyke until I reached the road. It was to be quite some time before I ventured there again.

Plate 2 Men clearing snow drifts, 1928/9.   (G)

Nowadays, sign-boards along part of the dyke give information about its history, excavations, its birds, flowers and wildlife. Amongst the flowers which have been found here are salad burnet, field fleawort, yellow rockrose, blue milkwort, eyebright, field scabious, harebell, bell flower, pink rest-harrow, sainfoin, wild pansies and violets, wild rose, purple milk vetch, mignonette, wild thyme and rare wild orchids. It is also a haven for bird watchers and among the birds which have been spotted here, are the skylark, corn bunting, turtle dove, yellow-hammer, long-tailed tit, whitethroat, sedge warbler, and the reed bunting.

Leaving the dyke and moving along the Swaffham Road amongst the first group of houses was the home of Mrs Badcock, caretaker of St. Mary's Church Parochial School, where my sister and I would often call on a Sunday after the morning service. She owned a dog and we would keep our scraps of food for it.

Plate 3. Railway station viewed from the Swaffham Road.

A field on the left of Heath Road, known as Margaret Field was left to the people of Burwell by Mrs Margaret O'Callaghan and named after her. At this junction of Swaffham Road, Heath Road and the High Street, the former railway bridge once stood and to the left of it the railway station. During the blackout of the Second World War the awkward turn on top of the bridge caused a number of

5

Plate 4. Stephenson's broken up old steam plough being loaded at railway station. (G)

Plate 5. Railway station and bridge.

6

Plate 6. The last goods train arriving at the railway station. (G)

Plate 7. Station yard and stationmaster's house. Courtesy Mrs F. Horton

vehicles to break through the barrier and roll down its banks. Mr Gates was in charge of the station at that time, and the cellar beneath his house was used as an air raid shelter. Passenger services were started on 2nd June 1884, and by 1886 there were five trains going

Plate 8. Signal man, Nelson Saunders. He made wheelbarrows, bags and boxes from scrap cars and sold them to raise money for the Baptist chapel. (G)

up to Cambridge from Mildenhall and five returning. By 1945 this was reduced to three each way. The train had two carriages and was affectionately known by the locals as the 'Mildenhall Express'. In addition to the regular train services there were a number of excursions and in 1937 a third class excursion ticket from Burwell to London cost four shillings and sixpence (twenty-two and a halfpence in today's currency), a half day excursion to Cambridge one shilling (five pence), an excursion ticket to Hunstanton, four shillings on a Sunday, and six shillings on a weekday. Freight going from here included fruit, vegetables, horses, cattle and flowers. As other forms of travel in Burwell became more popular there was a decline in the number of passengers using the railway and the last passenger train service ceased on 18th June 1962, and the line finally closed on 19th April 1965. The station, which on several occasions had won the competition for the best kept in Cambridgeshire, was demolished during October 1967 and the site now forms part of the premises of St. Regis' Packaging. The bridge was not demolished until July 1973 and some of the material was used for the construction of the Swaffham Prior by-pass. Incidentally in 1988 Burwell won the competition for the best kept village in East Cambridgeshire with over one thousand population.

St. Regis' Packaging was begun as a cottage industry by Mr Paske from Kentford, starting as Corrugated Fittings in the Primitive Methodist Chapel making strawberry baskets. The materials were delivered to the workers' homes and collected when the work was finished. After a fire the business moved to a barn behind Briarwood, a house in North Street, and was acquired by Tillotson's Corrugated Cases Ltd in 1956. It is now a major employer in the area and has received a number of design awards.

On the other side of the factory is Reach Road or as it was formerly shown on old maps, Scotred Lane. Leading off on the left of the road is Tan House Lane which as the names implies, leads to the Tan House, other names being Tanner's House, Tan Office, Newmarket Villa and Mandeville corner. It was once the home of a tanner, Isaac Brooks who died in 1664, and was later rented to a farmer John Miller, and then a maltster. The original part of the house goes back to the seventeenth century, with alterations and additions having been made over the years. Parts of it are of Georgian and Victorian construction. The house is built of clunch, brick and timber, there is a delightful pond in the garden, which was probably very useful for the tanner to soak his hides, although he may well have used the nearby stream in the Spring Close. I stayed in the house once with my mother when the Edwards family, for whom my mother did some sewing, were away and have visited its gardens on a number of occasions when the church has sometimes had its Annual Fete there. Dr Edwards was a research physiologist and his family Jersey cow was the first calf to be born in this country by artificial insemination. Francis Pym, at one time the Conservative Member of Parliament for Cambridgeshire, has also lived here.

The Manor House on the left of the High Street is another old house. Once the home of Salisbury Dunn, and more recently for many years, Colonel and Mrs O'Callaghan it was built about 1750. Mrs O'Callaghan was an American and some of the walls of the house were adorned with some rare American scenic wallpaper. She was an active worker for the Red Cross in the Chippenham division and on 15th May 1939 the Burwell Women's Detatchment, Cambridgeshire 66, was formed and met in 'the little room beside the kitchen'. It began with twenty four members under the Commandant, Mrs Geoffrey Scott. It was disbanded in 1969 although the Red Cross loan service still continues. The Burwell Red Cross Youth group began in 1976 and in 1979, Major R.H. Ratcliffe formed the Burwell Red Cross Centre, which serves Burwell, Cheveley, Dullingham, Kirtling, Saxon Street, Snailwell, Stetchworth and Wood Ditton.

Plate 9. The Manor House about 1930.   (G)

I well remember the figure of the little black boy standing at the foot of the steps to the Manor House, holding a lantern. At the side of the house are some old thatched barns, one of which has a conical shaped roof, an oast house and known as the Maltings. Unfortunately on July 26th this year a severe fire ripped through this complex causing an estimated £250,000 worth of damage, and took fire crews over four hours to control the blaze. There were eight other malting houses in Burwell, Carter's, Fuller's, the Parsonage, Harding's, one at Burnt Yard, two at Jerusalem opposite and one at 'Briarwood'. It was once likely to have been a very profitable industry. The oast house was where the grain was dried over a furnace. Nearby is a clunch built granary. One side of its roof took over three thousand bundles of reed to cover when it was rethatched in 1985 and is one of the oldest and best known landmarks in the village. Old maps of the High Street show a green with a pond somewhere in this area.

Plate 10. Oast house and old cottage about 1920.

Nearly opposite the Manor House is Isaacson's Road which leads to Exning and Newmarket. A lane to the left of this road leads to the now disused clunch pit which was one of several. Others were situated in Toyse Lane, Mill Lane and the parish pit on the Broads opposite the sewage works. This was used by the public for building walls and for road making, but has now been filled in with household waste. Some of the pits once belonged to the Gardiner family but the one off Isaacson Road belonged to the Carter family and was the last to close. In 1349 it provided material used in the Lady Chapel of Ely Cathedral, and in 1415 more was taken for Trinity College Gateway in Cambridge. Clunch from these pits was last used for Woburn Abbey and repairs to Anglesey Abbey, the last being cut in July 1962. Sometimes referred to as 'Burwell Rock' these blocks could be as much as twenty feet thick and were sometimes carved at the pit site instead of on the site where it was to be used.

Plate 11. The Carter family outside number 30 Reach Road in 1907. Left to right, back row: Ted, Rose, Jim; middle row: James, Robbie, May, Wal, Ethel, Jack, Jame's wife; front row: children, Ernie, Harry, and Lil.   Courtesy Miss Brenda Carter

Number 2 High Street, Harlech House, which stands on the corner of Isaacson's Road, affectionately known as Ennion's corner, and once known as Dunn's Malting Corner, was once the home of Dr Eric Ennion, the famous naturalist, artist and writer. Born in 1890 he moved to Burwell in 1906 where his father Octavius, an eighth child, and a doctor, had the house built. He practised here for twenty years. Following in his father's footsteps Eric also practised here for a further twenty years and I can remember him visiting me when I was ill in bed with whooping cough. He organized baby shows in the village during the early 1920s. In 1942 he wrote Adventurer's Fen, a book containing many sketches executed during his many visits to the fens. He went on to become a prolific writer, broadcaster and self taught painter, supplying many of his pictures for exhibitions and lectures. Amongst the books he wrote were: 'The British Bird', 'Animal Warfare', 'Life in Pond and Stream', 'The Story of Migration', 'Bird Life', 'Cambridgeshire and

Huntingdonshire', 'Bird Study in the Garden', 'The House on the Shore', 'Bird Watching', 'Shell Bird Book', and' Signals for Survival'. Some of these were written in collaboration with other writers. He also wrote many articles and series for a variety of magazines.

Plate 12. Carter's clunch pit. (G)

When Dr Ennion left Burwell Dr Robert Elliott came to Harlech House and was a Practitioner here for thirty four years until his retirement.

Isaacson Road was named after the Isaacson family who lived in the house at number 6 High Street, known as Isaacson's for over two hundred years. The last member of the family, a spinster named Mary died in March 1811. The house was probably built around 1348 and thought to be a hospice owned by the Order of Hospitallers and connected with the Priory of St. John of Jerusalem. Years ago when some restoration work was done three shields of stone were found. In the centre of these was a black cross formed of split black flintstone representing the shield of the Knights Hospitallers as distinct from that of the Knights Templars, which was a red cross on a white ground. The shield shows that at one time the house was in the possession of the Hospitallers. It would have been governed by a preceptor and four brethren, their duties being chiefly to minster to the wants of travellers, the poor, the sick and the needy.

Plate 13. Clunch Pits. (G)

Number 12 was for many years a general store where my mother worked for a short time.

On the opposite side of the road a little further along stand some thatched cottages which belonged to the late Dorothy Grainger who was well known for many years as the local photographer. Born in Yorkshire in 1894 she met her husband, Albert, a Burwell man, while he was stationed in the army, near to where she was working. She ran a dressmaking business and after meeting Sir Barnes Wallis she made all the covers for the airships for a firm in Blackpool because they had no girls to make them. Her husband started the photographic business in 1923 after marrying Dorothy and bringing her to Burwell, a photographer having just left the village. At first they lived with his family in Ness Road and then Albert became butler to Lord Glanely in Exning. They moved and rented number 17 High Street for one shilling and ninepence (about ninepence in today's currency) a week, from an elderly man at the Manor House.

Plate 14. Clunch Pits.   Courtesy Mr & Mrs E. Jacobs

Plate 15. 1842 tithe map of High Town. Photographed by the author while it was in the possession of Mr Jim Townsend.

Plate 16. Cottages in High Street with a flock of sheep, 1926.

Plate 17. Cottages in High Street, 1920. Courtesy Mrs F. Horton

Plate 19. The author's sister Pat and herself photographed by Mrs Grainger in the 1940s. Courtesy Mrs Mabel R. Johnson

Plate 18. Mrs Burling delivering milk from a churn in 1929.

Plate 20. Albert Grainger's brother Percy with grocer's cart outside Grainger's shop in the 1920s. The roadman is Harry Nunn.

Plate 21. Mrs Dorothy Grainger with an enlarger, 1956.

Plate 22. Cottages in High Street, 1920.   Courtesy Mrs F. Horton

When the row of four cottages came up for auction they bought them for one hundred and twenty pounds. In one of them an elderly man, Mr William Secrett, supplemented his parish relief of two shillings and sixpence per week by repairing clocks and watches. Dorothy carried on the business alone for a while until Lord Glanely was killed when a bomb dropped on his house in Weston-Super-Mare.

This put paid to Albert's job and he returned to the photographic business. They acquired a Kodak agency and the business flourished, gaining local, national and international interest. A cupboard under the stairs was used as the dark room and while Aladdin paraffin lamps provided light for printing, acetylene gas was used for enlarging. An enlarger was bought at an auction for five shillings and prints were washed in a large saucer bath rocked rhythmically to give movement. At first there was no mains water supply and the water had to be drawn from a well which was later modernised to include a pump. They began a postal service, but unfortunately sometimes the envelopes were too big for the local pillar box, so Dorothy would have to stand and wait, sometimes for quite a long while in snow or rain, for the postman who was invariably late. In 1926 Dorothy raised a petition to get a larger box to replace the smaller one. She was successful and came to regard box 344 as her own, but she was none too happy when it was temporarily moved during the demolition of the railway bridge as she had to tramp onto a messy bank to reach it.

Plate 23. The High Street in 1900.

At first their mode of travel was on a motorcycle, sometimes having as many as five weddings to attend on a Saturday as well as writing up all the reports for the local papers. When they sold the motorcycle after the second world war they travelled by bicycle or used the local bus service. Cameras ranged in price from five shillings to three pounds and an eight-exposure film cost one shilling.

Dorothy wrote for five local papers and was secretary and a founder member of the local women's branch of the British Legion, as well as running a lending library from her shop. She also belonged to the Exning branch of the Women's Institute and made several albeit fruitless attempts to found a branch in Burwell. Eventually with the help of some leaflets supplied by the Cambridge branch her campaign was successful and a preliminary meeting was held in December 1936. A Mrs Dunn became its first president and continued to be so for twenty three years. The first meetings were held in the Burwell Secondary Modern School by kind permission of Mr Glendon, the headmaster. By the time the branch was fifteen years old it had two hundred members. The Women's Institute celebrated their Golden Jubilee in 1987 and these celebrations culminated this year (1990) when they had raised enough funds to provide a beautifully carved oak sign which has been given to the people of Burwell and erected on the Pound Hill. Dorothy made contributions to the BBC, The Sunday/Daily Express, Garden News, Angling Times, and Motorcycling News, and did some work for Woburn Abbey, Anglia TV, the Royal Paddocks at Hampton Court, Blue Peter and the Oxford University Press. Amongst her many correspondents were Cyril Fletcher and Giles the cartoonist. Her hobbies, especially as she grew older included, needlework, embroidery and crochet and apparently she was also an excellent model for the art courses at Burwell House.

Plate 24. Mrs Grainger's cottage being thatched.

Plate 25. Mrs Grainger's shop window when she sold records. (G)

Plate 26. Gramophone repair man, 1929.

Plate 27. 'Stop me and buy one' in the High Street in the 1930s. (G)

Plate 28. Thatching Hill Farm in the High Street.

Plate 29. Mrs Dunn, President of the Women's Institute for 21 years, January 20 1938. (G)

Plate 30. January 20th 1938, Women's Institute's first Birthday cake. (G)

Plate 31. Women's Institute 'Olde Thyme Music Hall' in the 1940s, standing from left to right: Mrs Sealy, Mrs F. Cunnington, Mrs P.W. Doe, Miss A. Curtis, Mrs R. Badcock, Mrs Adams, Mrs H. Bridgeman, Mrs Mee; sitting Mrs Reg Hancock, Mrs M.R. Johnson (author's mother), Mrs Jennings, Mrs P. Goodchild, with Mrs Eric Smith at the piano. Courtesy Mrs Mabel R. Johnson

As a little girl I was taken along with my sister to her house to have our photograph taken. I was allowed to look under that mysterious black hood into the camera, and was somewhat startled to see my sister sitting upside-down. Shortly after Albert's death in 1952 she gave up the business and took pictures only as a hobby. One of these pictures stands out very clearly in my mind. In the early hours of 7th November, 1955, after what had been a day of almost tropical heat, my sister and I (and probably the rest of the village) were awakened by a terrifying sound of breaking glass, crashes and bangs. Waking to this unbelievable noise in the middle of the night, we felt we were in the middle of an air raid. As it became a little quieter we ventured down the stairs to be met in the hall by a broken window with hailstones and broken glass strewn everywhere. Many other panes were cracked and broken especially the lattice windows at the back of the house. There was much destruction in Burwell and the surrounding villages, including extensive damage to the Vicarage

Plate 32. Women's Institute group left to right standing: Miss Bertha Claydon, Miss Ford, Miss Gwendoline Johnson (author's aunt); seated: Miss Ada Claydon, Mrs Warren, Mrs Adams. Courtesy Mrs Mabel R. Johnson

Plate 33. Collection of hailstones after the storm on 7th November 1955. (G)
Courtesy Mrs Katie Hills

Plate 34. Mr Herbert Pryke with Mr Ken Bailey in background at Halesfield Nursery, Fordham, surveying the damage to the greenhouses after the storm, 7th November 1955.
Courtesy Mr Herbert Pryke.

Plate 35. Singing on the Vicarage lawn. (G)

27

Plate 36. Hurrell's the butchers in the High Street, 1925. (G)

Plate 37. Hurrell's the butchers in the High Street 1925. Left to right: Charlie Mutt, Jack Hurrell's sister Mrs Helen Holder, Morley Fordham (Newmarket's first taxi man), George Munns, Herbert Hurrell, Jack Hurrell, and Sid Hatley who was fatally scalded while working at a slaughterhouse in Newmarket. (G)

and Pembroke farm. Many windows were broken and not one house on the Newmarket Road escaped damage, with one council house alone having thirty nine broken panes. A market gardener had his seedlings torn out of the ground, cloches were smashed and the damage to his Dutch lights was estimated at two hundred and fifty pounds. The storm raged for over twenty minutes and most people had stories to tell of varying degrees of damage to homes and crops. The hailstones were reported to be as large as golf balls and not surprisingly a number of sparrows were found to have been killed.

Characteristically it was Dorothy who got up and collected a quantity of hailstones together, and with her half plate camera, made yet another unique photograph, six hundred copies of which were sold, excluding those which featured in newspaper articles. This helps to show how popular and well known her work was. Incidentally a similar incident occurred in 1728 early in the morning of 17th May at around 3 o'clock when there was a violent hailstorm. Three or four hours later when these hailstones were measured they were found to vary in size from two to three inches, by which time of course they had melted considerably.

Dorothy died on Christmas Day 1988 at the age of ninety five. Some of her cameras and other equipment are now in the Castle Museum at York and the War Museum at Duxford, while a collection of some of her photographs are in the Cambridge Collection, at the City Library in Cambridge. The B.B.C. made a film about her some thirty or forty years ago.

At number 21, Hill Farm, the yard was used as a coal yard. Nearly opposite stands the Vicarage where I have enjoyed many a church fête. Some of the activities included, skee-ball, bowling for the pig, feeding Hungry Harry, guessing the weight of the cake or box of fruit, and what time the clock stopped. There would be refreshments and maybe maypole dancing and singing by some of the school children.

Beyond this there is Lane's the bakers, an old established firm now about a hundred years old, where I used to collect my mother's bread. Recently during alterations to the house a five hundred year old fireplace was discovered and restored. Nearby was Ellis' the barbers, where in the 1960s I brought my sons from Cambridge for a haircut, which was then considerably cheaper than Cambridge prices. Tom Ellis' father came to Burwell in 1900 when he started the business. When Tom was fourteen, he was sent to

Liverpool for five years to learn the trade. His wages were two shillings a week. In 1946 he took over the business and also ran a newsagents on the premises. At first the papers were collected from the railway station and then later delivered by the Burwell and District bus company. Before he retired fifty years later, a van was delivering five hundred papers each evening. Almost next door is Hurrell's the butchers, another old established family firm and again over one hundred years old. In the days before electricity a Ford car was jacked up and used to supply power to the sausage machine.

Plate 38. High Town in the 1900s.   Courtesy Mrs F. Horton

    On the left is the Parish church of St. Mary the Virgin which dates back to the fifteenth century and was thought to have been completed in 1464 by the same builders who erected King's College Chapel in Cambridge. Over the chancel arch is an inscription in Latin which translated, says, 'Pray for the souls of John Benet, Johanna and Alice his wives, and his parents who caused to be made this wall and the carpentry work of this church AD 1464'. In the early 1800s an inhabitant of Burwell wrote a ballad:

'When the building of King's College Chapel was done,
Soon after it's workmen to Burwell did come.
There an elegant structure indeed they did raise,
Which to this very day may be seen, to their praise.

In length and in breadth well proportioned and high,
Its windows each other admirably high,
Its pillars most stately, and fine arches fair,
For lightness few churches can with it compare.

Plate 39. Drawing of St Mary's Church, 1743.

Originally, there were two churches, the other being that of St. Andrew's of which little is known. Each church was probably provided by a lord for two separate communities. St Andrew's was thought to be connected with Fordham Abbey and had a round tower. One statement proclaims that the West end was still standing in 1787, another that it was pulled down in 1664 when it fell into disrepair. Yet another states that it was pulled down by Henry Turner, Vicar here from 1772-1808, in order to make a paddock for his horse. Apparently he was not very bright but he is credited with presenting a Cambridge Borough manuscript to Caius College Library in Cambridge which had been stolen from the University many years before. The church was situated on the present site of St. Mary's Church School, and when it fell or was pulled down the two churches were amalgamated.

A report of 1743 claims that St. Mary's was in a 'decent, elegant order well paved and in the cleanest condition and that there was an estate in the parish of above fifty pounds per annum to keep it in repair'. The patronage of the living has been the responsibility of Cambridge University since 1545 and a sermon is preached annually in mid-Lent by the Vice-Chancellor or his deputy. In 1810 the then Vice-Chancellor Dr Gretton, accompanied by the Rev Robert Hole, Fellow of Trinity College, came to Burwell and preached. After the service they proceeded to the Manor House, the residence of Mr Salisbury Dunn the Churchwarden, where they partook of the usual substantial dinner with a liberal supply of ale and fine port. At the accustomed time the bells rang for the afternoon service, but all but the vicar, Mr Turner, turned a deaf ear. He departed to preach a sermon out of compliment to the Vice-Chancellor, expecting the rest of the party to follow in the carriage which was waiting . The Vice-Chancellor asked his host what sort of preacher Mr Turner was. The host replied that for his own part he would not set foot over the threshold to hear him preach. Dr Gretton decided to stay and have a few more glasses of port. After waiting a considerable time the Vicar had to proceed without him.

The original church of St. Mary was Saxon and nearby have been found remains of a Saxon burial ground. Vestries were added during the thirteenth and fourteenth centuries and the fire-engine was stored in one of these at one time. Among the parish records of 1745 I found an agreement for the purchase of a fire engine made of English oak of first size for twenty pounds, thirty foot of leather pipe with brass screws for three pounds three shillings, and strong substantial buckets at five shillings each. The receipt for transporting the fire engine from Newmarket was for two shillings and sixpence.

The upper part of the tower was probably built during the fifteenth century. Standing on one of the highest parts of the village it was used as a beacon and in the second world war was a useful lookout post. Six feet up in the tower are two worn carvings, one a king's head and the other the Prince of Wales feathers. A former Curate of the 1900s, Rev C.W. Millard was well known for his feat of climbing a steeplejack's ladder to touch the cockerel on the steeple.

Incidentally a cock for the weather vane cost five pounds and five shillings in 1908 and in 1748 a new clock cost forty six pounds.

Plate 40. St Mary's Church in the 1920s.   Courtesy Mrs F. Horton

During the year 1861 the church was closed for seven months (services being held in the boys' school) while it was thoroughly restored. The main part of the roof had already been releaded and restored the previous year. Now the roof of the north aisle underwent the same restoration. The old square pews were mostly removed and new oak pews sited and added to, raising the seating capacity to three hundred and fifty and these were now free. The west arch, which had been boarded up for some time, was thrown open, and a gallery or singing pew was erected across it, the ringer's floor removed and the tower opened into the church. This now houses eight bells although for two or three hundred years it only had five, four of which were provided by Richard Keene of Royston in 1703, and the fifth a tenor was added by Thomas Newman of Cambridge in 1725. Arthur Mason, a London ringer who originated from Burwell paid for these bells to be restored as well as for three new ones to be added, these being cast by John Taylor & Co. from Loughborough. Writing about the bells reminds me of the time when I used to watch

Mr Stanley Faircliffe the sexton ringing three bells by himself—he would loop one rope round one foot and ring one with each hand. Later when a team evolved I became a ringer but after first breaking a stay while ringing in the church at Swaffham Prior and then another in this church I decided I was a bit of a liability and so turned my hand to handbell ringing for a time. Since then new handbells have been acquired.

The floor was laid with black and red Staffordshire tiles and a new pulpit and reading desk installed. Outside the church an efficient drainage system was carried out to prevent the progress of decay and internal damp. The church was re-opened on Wednesday 12th February 1862.

Later, in 1877 further restoration work was carried out, this time to the chancel. A new reredos of carved clunch cut from quarries in the parish was erected through the liberality of the University and the old oak screen was restored. The 'Hall pew', a commodious square pew over the north door which commanded a view of the whole church, was taken down. A new two manual organ of seven hundred pipes was installed in the Chancel at a cost of three hundred pounds, and at the dedication service was played by Mr Bevington from Messrs Bevington of London, the suppliers.

Taking as his text I Kings 6:7 'in building the temple, only blocks dressed at the quarry were used, and no hammer, chisel, or any other iron tool was heard at the temple site while it was being built', the Bishop of the Diocese preached at the 11.30 morning service. He urged his hearers to remember that 'though God was pleased to honour his earthly temples of stone with His favour and presence, yet they themselves were the temples of the Living God'. After Matins there was a celebration of Holy Communion attended by many of the neighbouring clergy and a large number of communicants. A luncheon was then provided in the boys' schoolroom. Toasts and speeches followed in which the Archdeacon extolled the virtues of the Rev. Cockshott (vicar from 1858-1885) who on arriving here found a dilapidated church and scanty school accommodation.

At Evensong celebrated at three o'clock the preacher Rev. F. Watson, Fellow of St. John's College, took as his text a portion of Revelation 21, descriptive of the new Jerusalem, which drew much interest from his congregation. A second evensong was held at 7 p.m. for labourers and others. The village choir assisted efficiently throughout the day and the services were well attended. The restoration was now complete with the exception of six life-size statues intended for the beautiful Gothic niches in the chancel. But these had unfortunately been lost or destroyed.

The first mention I could find of an organ was in 1556 when fourpence was charged for its repair. In 1820, a barrel organ was sited at the west end of the chancel, parts of which are thought to have been incorporated into the organ at St. Andrew's church when it was removed from St. Mary's in 1862. The next organ seems for a short time to have stood where the pulpit now stands. Before the days of electricity in 1866 John Davey was paid ten shillings for 'blowing the organ'. The instrument which preceded the present one was in the Chancel where I received my organ lessons from Mr Arthur King. The present organ was installed in 1967, dedicated by the Bishop of Huntingdon and was placed at the west end of the church. It took three thousand hours to build and was thought to be worth ten thousand pounds at the time of its completion.

A flight of steps to the North of the chancel leads down to a crypt. In the recess of its east wall rests an altar or podium of stone while on the north wall is a fireplace. Although now divided by a modern partition it was generally supposed that this crypt had been a private chapel connected with the Abbey of Ramsey and is locally known as 'Monk's Hole.' It was once used as a vestry and in 1743 several old iron helmets were found hanging there.

The old rood screen was higher than the present one and had two doorways, one of which is now boarded up. Hidden under the carpet of the chancel is a brass figure in Abbot's vestments representing John Lawrence de Warboys, who served as last Abbot of Ramsey from 1508-1539. After the dissolution of the Abbey, the brass was cut in two, the top half being renewed and the lower half turned over and engraved, showing the abbot in plain clerical attire. The figure stood under a triple canopy of which only the centre remains. The reverse side of the canopy shows fragments of another figure of the much earlier date of 1325, probably a deacon, and unique of its kind. As no brass plate was manufactured in England before 1639 it was probably a fragment brought ready engraved from abroad. It is now secured to the floor but a cast of the underside can be seen on the wall by the crypt door. Behind the altar is a reredos of mosaics depicting the scenes of the Annunciation, the Wedding of Cana and The Visitation.

Plate 41, 42. St Mary's Church in the 1920s. Courtesy Mrs F. Horton

36

Plate 44. Palimpset Brass of Effigy, 1935.
Courtesy Cambridge Antiquarian Society

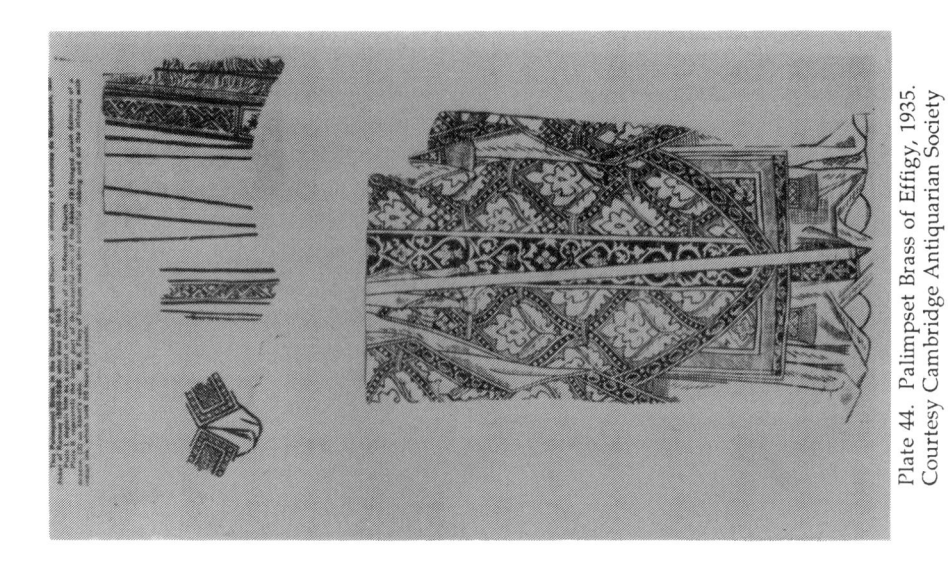

Plate 43. Palimpset Brass of Abbott, 1935.
Courtesy Cambridge Antiquarian Society

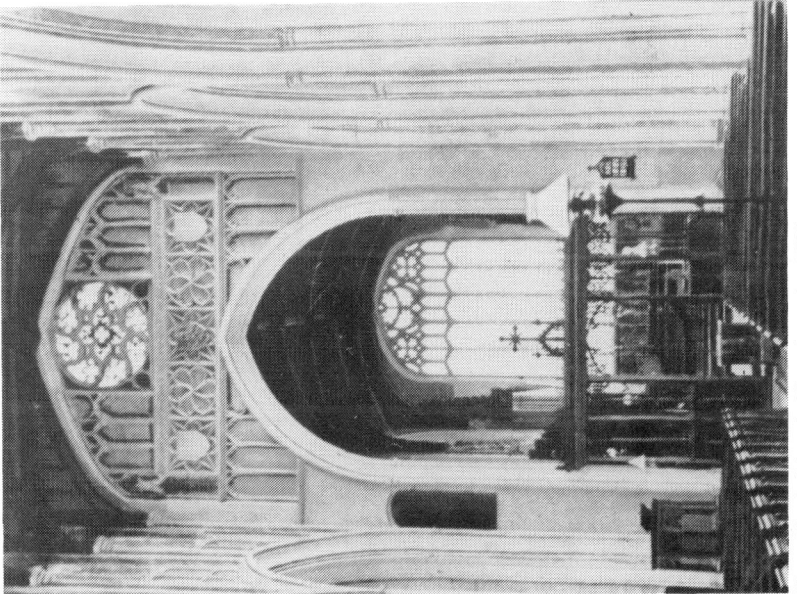

Plate 45. St Mary's Church in the 1920s.
Courtesy Mrs F. Horton

Plate 46. Repairing the church clock. (G)

Plate 48. Collecting waste paper for the girl's choir in 1957, Brenda Carter and Elizabeth Bridgeman. Mrs Heather M. Richardson

Plate 47. Church war memorial. (G)

Above the centre arch can be seen a rose window showing the Marys of the Bible. This was installed by Rev. Cockshott in memory of his daughter Ethel who died abroad at a German college, and on either side of the wooden screen are two stained glass windows erected in 1934. The one on the north aisle depicts the Adoration of the Wise Men and the Annunciation while that on the south aisle shows the Visitation of Mary to Elizabeth and the infant Christ presented in the Temple. There are several monuments, one dedicated to the Russell family, one to Lady Russell dated 1717, who lived at the Parsonage, four to Isaacsons' descendants, and one carved in clunch from the Burwell quarry to Robert Bridgeman, who became a great architect, church restorer and sculptor. He was born in Burwell, orphaned and brought up by relatives. He started work at a firm in Peterborough and was then sent to Lichfield Cathedral. Here he carved sixty-one of the one hundred and thirteen beautifully carved statues around the Cathedral and twice became Lord Mayor. He died in 1918. On the north wall is an old medieval wall painting of St. Christopher.

During Canon Walpole Sayer's time, (1921-44) while a grave was being dug to the north-east of the graveyard, evidence was found of the top of an arch which was thought to be an entrance to a tunnel and only a few years ago some slabbing gave way at Isaacson's house exposing an entrance to another tunnel. It is very probable that tunnels connected the church with the castle and Isaacson's house.

Burwell has had a long history of choral singing and festivals. On July 4th in 1863 one such festival was held here in conjunction with the Church Music Society, for the local parishes of Burwell, Cheveley, Fordham, Ickworth, Exning, Soham, Wicken and Wood Ditton. The music was directed by the Reverend F.H. Gray, Chaplain of King's College and one hundred and sixty six singers took part. The organ was played by Mr H. Brown, organist of Trinity Church and Jesus College, Cambridge. Flags were flying, the bells were rung and Soham band took part in the celebrations. After one hour's rehearsal a service took place at 3 o'clock. The choristers were joined by clergy and friends for tea in the boys' school and a second service was held during the evening which was more packed than that of the afternoon.

At a church festival in June twelve years later the Dean of Ely preached an interesting sermon on 'Excuses for not attending church', these were: 1. prays at home, 2. not a scholar, 3. did not understand the clergy, 4. service too long. Although he acknowledged some clergy were at fault, he took as his text Luke 14.18 'but they all alike began to make excuses. The first said, I have just bought a field, and I must go and see it, please excuse me'; and he spoke of people preferring to seek this world instead of the Kingdom of Heaven. Afterwards he praised the vicar of St. Mary's, the Rev. Cockshott for all he had done by hard work and said that Burwell was morally and spiritually a very different place from what it had been twenty year's earlier.

Plate 49. New choir robes, December 1957. Back row, left to right: Jennifer Sargeant, Wendy Barton, Ann Carter, Jennifer Faircliffe, Heather Johnson; front row: Daphne Carter, Elizabeth Bridgeman, Maureen Lawrence, Pat Johnson, Brenda Carter and Violet Hills.   Mrs Heather M. Richardson

A choir supper on 9th January 1868 was held in the boys' school for the choir and their friends. Fifty six people partook of roast beef, roast shoulder of lamb and potatoes, boiled leg of mutton and turnips, cheese and celery, and plum pudding. The men then sat down with their pipes while the children played games. Men who had been working on the restoration of the chancel then joined them and the younger people had sweet wine, nuts, oranges and figs. At nine o'clock mince-pies were served and the evening finished with the singing of Keble's evening hymn.

Plate 50. Visit of the Vice Chancellor in the 1920s: second row left to right Walpole Sayer, Vice Chancellor, ? with Fred Cowles at the back (a distant relative of the author). Courtesy Cambridge County Record Office

At a choral festival in 1871 the following was overheard, 'if Mr Cockshott had been here fifty years ago there would have been no chapels, for everyone must be struck with the earnestness of the clergy and the piety of their people'. In October at the Harvest Festival service of the same year Rev. Cockshott said that he 'hoped the farmers would join together for one feast for harvest labourers when they meet together before God to return thanks instead of each giving a separate "horky" (feast or supper) which so often ended in drunkenness and debauchery'.

When my father and his family moved to Burwell from Newmarket in 1926 he and his brother joined the church choir. I followed in this tradition when I went to the Burwell Secondary School, and became a founder member of the female section, often taking the solo part of an anthem sung at Whitsuntide or Harvest. The ladies of the choir were unable to process with the men and boys as the church could not afford to buy robes for us, so we decided to raise the money ourselves. Probably the most successful fund raising effort was the income we received from collecting old newspapers which we would pile onto a borrowed barrow and store in my Aunt's garage on Ness Road until enough had accumulated to warrant a collection from the waste paper unit. After almost a year the princely sum of ninety one pounds and sixteen shillings had been raised and after a meeting held at the vicarage where we were allowed to voice our opinion as regards colour and style, ten sets of blue robes and surplices were duly purchased on our behalf. On Christmas Day 1957 we made our first robed entry. A large wardrobe was installed in the South porch which we then used as our vestry. We received ten shillings (fifty pence in today's currency) at Christmas and Whitsun from a trust called the Robert Henry Maloney Trust left by his sister for 'well behaved choirboys'.

Plate 51. St. Mary's Church, 1990 showing the organ at the West end.
Mr John G. Richardson

The earliest mention I could find of a Sunday School treat was one reported on 23rd July 1859 in the Burwell Chronicles. Prayers were said and an appropriate address was given in church by Rev. O.T. Thorpe. Under the auspices of him and his lady, the ladies of the committee and the Burwell Band, the children processed from the church with their teachers to the Spring Close singing hymns as they went. Tea and cake were supplied in abundance followed by a variety of amusements and 'loyalty to the Queen was not forgotten'. When I first went to Sunday School during the second World War it was held in a classroom in St. Mary's Junior school attended by only five children. Later, when it expanded we moved into the Guildhall with Miss Swann as the superintendent. As I grew older I played the piano to accompany the hymns and choruses and later became one of the Sunday School teachers taking a class of the very smallest children. During the war we received national saving stamps as an annual prize. After the war books were presented to those with a record of full attendance. As treats, day trips took us to places like Wicksteed Park in Kettering or to Hunstanton, or Bury St. Edmunds, travelling on the Burwell and District buses.

Plate 52. The old bier, 1990.   Mr John Richardson

At the age of fifteen I was prepared for confirmation by the Reverend Cripps (1944-54) and later confirmed in Burwell church by the then Bishop of Ely, but alas, my knowledge of the Lord Jesus was sadly lacking and it was to be many years later before I understood that the only way to God was through Jesus, God's Son, that He was our Saviour and that He loved us so much that He died for us, for He says in the Bible, 'I am the Way the Truth and the Life. No-one comes to the Father except by Me.'

Of course there have been many records made of the accounts of Burwell church but it might be interesting to note that according to a lecture given by the Rev. Walpole Sayer, some of the expenses from an old churchwarden's book include payments made of three shillings and fourpence, or six shillings and eightpence for a fox, according to its sex, two shillings for a pole cat, one shilling for a weasel and threepence for a hedgehog. In 1823 as much as fifteen pounds was paid for sparrows' eggs, pole cats and weasels. By 1846 these items ceased being mentioned. Before electricity was installed of course there was no heating in the church and no evening service.

Another document which I found interesting was a church magazine of July 1887, priced at one penny, in which there was an article about Jubilee Day, and I thought it might be of interest to quote from it in full:

> 'Jubilee Day' was on the whole a happy day for the inhabitants of Burwell. Although there was a good deal of disappointment arising from the fact that, owing to the Jubilee Funds being devoted to building a Reading-Room as a memorial of this happy time, there was no general dinner or tea for all the inhabitants, as was, we believe, the case in most of the neighbouring villages, yet as people began to understand that there was not money enough in the place for a dinner *and* a Reading-Room, they got over their disappointment and joined heartily in the amusement provided for them. The day began in Burwell by a Celebration of the Holy Communion in the Parish Church at 7.30 a.m. This was followed at 11 a.m. by the special Service prepared by the Archbishop of Canterbury, and which was, we are glad to say a "United Jubilee Thanksgiving", for Nonconformists joined with Churchmen in the old walls of the Mother Church at Burwell in offering praises to God for the completion of fifty years of Her Majesty's reign. The prayers were intoned by the Rev. W.J. Wickins, the lesson was read by the Minister of the High Town Meeting House, while the sermon was preached by the Vicar on the text, Levit. 25.11, "A Jubilee shall that fiftieth year be unto you". The Service was most hearty throughout, and we are glad that the Nonconformists of the various denominations in the village were able and willing to accept the invitation given them by the Vicar to join in united

praise and thanksgiving. At 2.30 p.m. there was a cricket match in the Park Close between the Married and Single, in which the former gained the victory. At 5 p.m. or thereabouts began the sports on the same ground, which were under the direction of an able Committee, and which afforded much amusement to the many competitors and on-lookers. The Burwell Band was in attendance and did much towards making the day pass off pleasantly; it has greatly improved in its playing, and we hope that after another winter's regular practice it will be as good as any of the Bands around, and will blossom out next summer into a uniform. Tea and coffee were given away to all who wished for them by the kindness of Mrs Salisbury Ball. Shortly before ten there was a display of fireworks, which was continued till near midnight. We felt somewhat ashamed that while the village street was well decorated with flags the Church Tower was bare. Will some of our readers present the Church with a proper flagstaff and flag, that in future we may be able to display the loyalty and the gladness which we feel on any occasion of national joy? Arrangements have been made by a Committee of ladies to give a meat tea to the people who are 68 and over (the Queen's age) also to those in receipt of parish relief; this tea is fixed for Thursday, June 23rd, and we hope all will go off well and the old folks be made happy'.

During Rev. James Johnson Baine's time (1808-54) the church was filled with square pews and there was a broad alley way up the middle of the nave. The school children sat either side on forms. When the Vicar came from the vestry in voluminous surplice and scarf, hood and bands, he proceeded up the church and the girls had to curtsy and the boys pulled their forelocks. To omit these courtesies would call forth a stern reprimand from the Vicar. He would be followed by the clerk wearing fawn coloured small clothes and gaiters, a black coat with large flap pockets, and white stock and cravat. After seeing the Vicar in he would fasten the door of the reading desk before going to his own place from where he announced any parish notices, sales, meetings and fairs. After the prayers the Vicar was escorted back down the church to the vestry to put on his black gown, and then to the pulpit by the clerk, who opened the pulpit door and shut the Vicar in.

One morning he was preaching on Baptism, a subject on which all were aware of his very pronounced views. But this particular morning the views he expressed were totally different from usual and it was apparent that he did not understand what he was preaching. According to Dr Lucas he belonged to the 'high and dry' church party while the Lucas' family were Evangelicals and held the views of Simeon and Canon Clayton which prompted Mrs Thomas Lucas to say often 'that Mr Baines was quite in the dark'. While on a fortnights holiday the unfortunate vicar had bought the sermon and had not read it through before preaching.

In 1837 Mr Baines, or 'Parson Baines' as he was locally known, was in trouble about the charities not being properly administered. The quarterly meetings were seldom held and the accounts not properly kept. He had subscribed twenty pounds in his own name out of the charity money to Addenbrooke's Hospital which made him a life governor. At a public enquiry held in Cambridge it was disclosed that he had paid public money into his own private account amounting over some years to four or five hundred pounds. Mr Edward Ball knew that the accounts had not been properly kept and that Mike Bailey had been instructed to cook the accounts for the occasion. When Mr Ball held up one of the pages to the light, sums apparently recorded in 1820 had been written on paper bearing a watermark of 1836. At this, Mr Baines fainted and Mike Bailey lost control of himself and had to leave the court. When Mr Baines refused to repay twenty pounds to Addenbrooke's Hospital, the charity was put in the care of the court. He had a fixed idea that he was not dishonest but thought the money was safer in his own account. As he lay on his death bed five hundred pounds of public money rested in his private account at the bank; it was with great difficulty that he was persuaded to write a cheque to restore it.

According to the old registers of the parish, the first recorded baptism was of Thomas Mannynge on 15th April, 1562, the first marriage was between John Wilkin and Alice Perfrey, a widow, on May 2nd 1563 and the first burial was that of John Rolfe on 21st April 1560. In 1786 on the 6th July, Elizabeth Hunt a pauper from the workhouse who had been murdered two days previously was buried. She was found about half a mile from Reach with her throat cut quite through to the bone. George Miller, a waterman was tried and found guilty of her murder at the next assizes. He was executed and his body was given to the surgeons to be anatomised. A much earlier murder occurred in 1272 when Agnes, the wife of Henry Silverlak was found dead near 'Borewell Mill'. He killed her in the twilight and then placed himself in the parish church.

Among the occupations from 1725 the records show there were, oatmealmakers, shoemakers, maltsters, basket makers, thatchers, barbers, carpenters, shepherds, watermen, bricklayers, masons, taylors, officer of excise, wheelwrights, cordwainers, knackers, poulterers, limeburners and from 1746 woolcombers, surgeon (female) alehousekeepers, collarmakers, ragmen and chimney sweep.

In 1854 the Crimean war began and one can only assume that this was the reason that Burwell held a 'Day of Humiliation', which was reported in the Cambridge Chronicles on 13th May as follows:-

> 'The Day of Humiliation. The manner in which the recent day of humiliation and prayer was kept in this parish deserves notice. Not only were all business matters suspended, but the inhabitants seemed to vie with each other in keeping it sacred and holy. All places of public worship were opened for services, and filled with crowded congregations. There were three services in the church, half-past nine in the morning, half past twelve midday, and half-past five in the evening—and thence did those hallowed walls resound to the prayers and praises of a numerous congregation. Two very earnest and impressive sermons were preached by the Reverend Thorpe of Christ's College, Cambridge, (mid-day and evening), which were listened to with almost breathless attention - and collections were made at the doors after each sermon for the soldier's widow and orphan fund, amounting in all to £6. 11s. $9^{1/4}$d and was in pence and half-pence.

There are several old tombstones from the 1700s in the churchyard but the most tragic, dated 1727 is called the Flaming Heart; it commemorates the death of seventy eight people. In the eighteenth century a fair—Stourbridge Fair—was held annually in Cambridge, an event which lasted a month and was a highlight of those days. Many traders and stallholders travelled some distance to be there. It was thought that a puppeteer, with his wife, daughter, and servant were making their way to this fair through Burwell when they found themselves short of funds to continue their journey. They decided to put on a small show in a barn which they hired in Cockles Row, somewhere near the present pharmacy. It must have caused quite a stir and the word soon spread. The barn, a clunch building with nine foot high walls and a thatched roof, was full of new dry straw and dried up old cobwebs. About one hundred and forty people crammed into the fifteen by seventeen foot space left available for the puppeteer and his audience. Many others wanted to get in but as there was no more room the door was locked. And so on September 8th at 9 o'clock the show began, the audience being charged one penny each. On searching the Cambridge Chronicles in the Archives at the Cambridge City Library I came across the following account which was copied in 1884 from a manuscript dated 1727 and which differs a little from the account often used.

> 'Extraordinary Accident at Burwell. - We copy from an old manuscript the following account of a frightful calamity which occurred at Burwell, in this county more than a century ago:- "September 9th, 1727. At Burwell in Cambridgeshire a Puppet Show was exhibited in a barn, ye doors were locked, and there was a stable adjoining to it where a boy was got with design to see it, for which purpose he climbed up upon some beams and took his candle with him, while he was viewing ye show fell down amongst a heap of straw and find it alight which ye boy perceiving he sprung out and narrowly escaped. The fire burning very fierce had catcht ye roof of this barn before ye people perceived it, ye doors were lockt to keep people out, and with some difficulty ye doors were broke and some escaped - but the rest pushing to get out wedged one another in yet none could stir till the roof fell in and 105 persons perished in ye flames. Some few were escapd into an adjoining yard which was built round with thatcht houses and on fire, but were forced to lie down and perish in it. An excise man and his child perished there and his wife is since quite distracted. After the fire was abated they found here an arm and there a leg, here a head there a body, some burnt with their bowels hanging out, most deplorable sight. There were abundance of people from the adjacent towns in ye number all most young persons"'.

A similar report from the burial register is kept in the County Records office and gives the names of the victims. Like the gravestone, this report states that seventy eight people perished on the same day and that two victims died the next day from their burns. It also states that a servant who started the fire had set a candle and lantern in or near the heap of straw. The servant, Richard Whitaker of the parish of Hadstock near Linton was tried at the next Assizes but because of lack of evidence was acquitted. In fact it appears he was the first to raise the alarm. The victims came from Reche (Reach) Swaffham Prior and Upware and the Excise officer and his wife, from Derbyshire. The puppeteer, his wife, daughter and manservant also perished. Several people were saved by Thomas Dobedee, a Wicken man. He broke down the door and dragged out as many people as he could. One of them had metal buttons on his breeches which had melted in the heat. Apart from two children who were buried in the Palmer vault, the bodies, some of whom had lost their heads, were transported in carts and buried in two pits.

Upon a very mournful occasion soon after a sermon was preached by the Rev. Alexander Edmondson, (1725-33) vicar of the parish. His text was taken from Lamentations 4:8: 'Their visage is blacker than a coal: they are not known in the streets: their skin cleaveth to their bones: it is withered, it is become like a stick'. A number of children among the victims it seems had climbed out of their bedroom windows to see the show. With a probable eight hundred inhabitants in the village at that time very many families would have suffered.

Over forty years after this event in February 1774 an old man lay on his deathbed perturbed. With great difficulty he told his friends and relatives that he had a confession to make. He proceeded to confess that he, an ostler at the time and with a grudge against the puppeteer, had set light to the barn at Burwell on September 8th 1727. He had started the fire in order to ruin the show not realising that the door had been locked. With death so near, sheer horror of his deed preyed on his mind and his passing was not exactly peaceful. I came across the following epitaph:

> They lie beneath the self same sod
> In Burwell churchyard lone,
> A burning heart is plain to see,
> All on a graveyard stone.
> Then let us sing, long live the King
> And Heaven's deliverance send
> From deadly blaze and foreign plays,
> And here my song doth end.

A booklet written by Rev. Thomas Gibbons D.D. who acquired his information from a man who was nine years old at the time of the fire was published in London in 1769 and a typed copy of it amounts to fifteen foolscap pages. This account is consistent with other accounts, but expounds the theory that it was an act of God. In September 1910 the stone was cleaned and inscribed as shown in plate 54.

Plate 53. Drawing of the barn where the fire took place
Courtesy Cambridge Antiquarian Society.

Plate 54. The flaming heart gravestone.　　　　Courtesy Mrs Wallis

51

Plate 55. The clock sun-dial in the churchyard, 1990.
Mr John Richardson

Plate 56. The face of the sun-dial, 1990.
Mr John Richardson

Another item of interest on the south side of the church in the churchyard is one of the oldest form of clocks, a sundial, or to give it its correct name, a scratch dial being cut or scratched on a block of stone. This one probably dates back to the twelfth century.

Growing up in Burwell I used to particularly enjoy the church parades, one of which was held to celebrate Armistice Day. The sound of the approaching band would thrill me as we sat in church awaiting its arrival. If I had been taking part as a brownie or later as a girl guide I would have been marching behind the band with the British Legion, Red Cross, Scouts, Cubs and many other organisations. Quite a long parade it seemed to me in those days. If not taking part I would hurry out of church after the service in order to be in time to walk beside the participants when we would all make our way to the War Memorial for a short service.

Church parades existed long before these times. According to records in the Cambridge Chronicles annual Church parades began in 1900. The second of these was held on August 4th 1901. As in the previous year, collections were made on behalf of Addenbrooke's Hospital, with an even larger number of people from the surrounding villages in attendance. It was organized and managed by a committee of representatives from various friendly societies. The parade started at the north end of the village at 5 p.m. and was headed by Burwell Band ably assisted by ten members of the Soham band. A large banner carried and belonging to the order of Shepherds followed and behind them the local Order of Shepherdesses in their regalia. Following on were the fire brigades from the Newmarket Jockey Club Owner' and Trainer' Brigade, a contingent from Fordham and nine members from Soham. These were followed by members of the Shepherds of Goshen Lodge of the Ancient Shepherds, which incidentally came into existence in 1845 and at their fiftieth Anniversary sat down to an excellent dinner and a good supper at the Anchor Inn. Members of Reach Lodge also came and The Anchor of Hope Benefit Society, and representatives of the Ancient Order of Foresters from Newmarket. Other Societies included Oddfellows, the Hearts of Oak and the Royal Standard Benefit Societies. They processed along the length of the village arriving at the church at 6.15 p.m. The building was crowded to the doors. The processional hymns were 'Onward Christian Soldiers', and 'Sons of Labour'. The Vicar preached from Psalm 104:23, 'Man goeth forth to his work and to his labour, until the evening'. Miss A. Lucas (sister of Charles

Lucas) played voluntaries on the organ before the service and Miss Powell played for the actual service, after which the procession reformed and marched to the large open space at the end of the Causeway and arranged themselves in a circle. Mr Harries, the chairman of the committee thanked all the visitors for being present and a verse of the national anthem was sung. The fourteen young ladies who had taken collections had worn sashes lent to them by Addenbrookes Hospital.

Plate 57. The blessing of the plough in 1969.

From 1961-70 when Rev. Haynes was the vicar, he and young members of the church made their own palm crosses for several years thus raising funds for the Church Missionary Society. The leaves came from a London supplier who imported them from the Middle East, each frond making two crosses.

New gates, made in 1890 were erected to the entrance of the churchyard to celebrate the quincentenary in 1964. The blessing of the plough was renewed in 1962 and was televised for Anglia television and although the tradition still continues it now takes place at the Baptist church.

Before the churchyard was extended on the North side of the church in 1859 at a cost of four hundred and thirty five pounds, a number of ruined cottages, probably almshouses, were removed as well as the old guildhall, which had been given to the village by Sir Edward Chester in 1555. Erected in the fifteenth century it was a large two-storey timber built house with a red flat tiled roof. A fourteen to fifteen foot wide passage which closed with a large black oak gate, probably a lychgate, extended under the whole width of the second floor and spanned the church path. This would have been very useful in those days as a resting place and shelter for the funeral bearers, especially if they came from the other end of the village or the weather was bad, and also if the person to be buried had died from cholera, smallpox or typhus fever. Typhus fever was very prevalent up to 1856 and the corpse may well have been left at the lychgate during the service. I found a receipt of 1743 for a bier, possible the old one which now stands at the back of the church, costing one pound and four shillings.

On the ground floor of the Guildhall there were large rooms and a large kitchen area. On the next floor was a very large assembly room capable of holding a great many people. Opposite this room was another large room and to the left was a staircase leading to the garrets Opposite the staircase was a large room over the kitchen in the centre of which was an oak post which was the whipping post used for disciplinary purposes when the Hall was used as a workhouse. According to notes left by Charles Lucas one village character, Dinah Pleasance lived in one of the almshouses nearby but spent her early days in the workhouse. She was not very bright and for some breach of discipline the Master stamped on her feet with such violence that she could only hobble and was crippled for life. Dinah was always neatly dressed and wore a brown gown, white apron, a black hooded cap bound with white and over her shoulders she wore a lacy bright scarlet cloak. She was by profession a letter carrier for Mark Bailey, who was the postmaster, village letter writer, newsmonger, and Parson Baine's factotum. She had many kind friends and because she could not read she went to the houses where she was told to go and people sorted out their own mail, at the same time supplying her with dumplings or broken food, which would be put in her basket along with the letters often leaving the envelopes somewhat greasy and evil smelling.

The Assembly room was used on weekdays for all the public meetings and entertainments. On Sundays under the supervision of the Vicar, it was used to teach religious instruction. Some of the rooms were used as a school for boys under the mastership of a hunchback, John Medbury who also lead the church singers from his tuneful barrel-organ.

After the appointment of Rev. J.W. Cockshott as Vicar, the Feoffees (Church Lands Charity Trust) were asked to renovate the Guildhall, modernising it to fit the requirements of a boys' school. The Feoffees thought a local builder's estimate of three hundred pounds too costly but the Charity Commissioners gave permission for the erection of a new building.

When the old guildhall was pulled down in 1859 the materials were sold and the proceeds used towards the cost of the new one. The old almshouses were pulled down and in June of that year at a confirmation service for forty four Burwell candidates and twenty from the surrounding villages the Lord Bishop of Ely consecrated this piece of ground to be incorporated into the churchyard as an additional burial ground. The bells rang merry peals throughout the day. The foundation stone of the new guildhall was laid on a piece of land the other side of the church on 28th June 1860. The building was intended as a new Guildhall and a school for ninety boys. The Feoffees held their meetings in the Committee room, and Dr Charles Lucas' father, who was a member during this time, served for forty years. His son carried on the tradition and also served for forty years. My father's brother, Leslie Johnson also served for many years.

The Guildhall has been the focal point of many other activities. The first parish meeting was held on 2nd January 1863 when two hundred parishioners, rich and poor had tea in the schoolroom. Tickets cost ninepence each and the walls were decorated; there was singing and addresses were given by Rev. Charles Clayton, Incumbent of Holy Trinity Cambridge, Rev. Thomas Preston, Vicar of Swaffham Prior, Rev. John Bell, Vicar of Fordham and Rev. M. Wilson, Rector of Teversham. Rev. Cockshott gave a detailed account of collections, services, visiting, cottage lectures, night schools and the hopeful work of a North Street mission church. It was enjoyed so much that it was thought it could be held at the beginning of each year. The next day a concert was held attended by three hundred people and the proceeds, together with the collections of the two previous Sundays amounted to ten pounds, eleven shillings and were given to aid the poor of Burwell and Lancashire. Even when the weather was bad 'penny readings' which were interspersed with music were well attended. The Guildhall also housed the Vicar's Mothers' meetings, clothing clubs, elections and Sol Far singing classes.

Plate 58. Mothers' Union in 1930s Back row left to right: Mrs Barton, Mrs Blythe, Mrs Rollo, Mrs Ennion, ?, Mrs Johnson (author's paternal grandmother), Mrs Parr, Mrs Sayer, Rev Walpole Sayer, and curate; middle row: Mrs Bray, Mrs Reeve, Mrs Wright, ?, ?, ?, ?, ?, ?, ?, Mrs Goodchild; front row: Mrs Ridgeon, ?, ?, ?, ?, ?, Mrs Bridgeman, Mrs Thackeray, and Miss Lucas. Courtesy Mrs Olive Johnson (author's aunt)

My own recollections of it consist of Sunday School and tea parties, C.M.S. slide shows, Brownies, Girl Guides and church meetings. Although it had been closed as a boys' school, it was reopened at the beginning of the Second World War to house child evacuees. I started school here when the infant teacher was a Miss Howlett who took her class in the small committee room. The next class up was taken by Miss Mary Parr. All classes were mixed and formed part of St. Mary's Church of England School situated across the road under the headship of Miss Florence Carter.

Plate 59. Scout parade 1920-30, leading Leslie E. Johnson (author's Uncle), second row far right: Ernie Gathercole, his brother Albert with glasses five rows back.
Courtesy Mrs Olive Johnson

Plate 60. Scout camp at Heacham 1920-30, back row left to right: Leslie E. Johnson, Wilfred H. Johnson (author's father); middle row: ?, Ernie Gathercole, ?, Albert Gathercole, ?
Courtesy Mrs Olive Johnson

Plate 61. Boys' school, May 12th 1919, back row left to right: Miss Gregory, R. Mansfield, L. King, C. Ransome, B. Hancock, J. Collins, I. Harries (Headmaster); middle row: C. Badcock, B. Peachey, S. Warren, S. Heffer, A. Barton; front row: A. Baker, Langley, R. Harding, B. Heeks, G. Fuller.

Plate 62. The present Guildhall, 1990   Mr John Richardson

Plate 63. Girl Guide group in the Spring Close, middle row: ?, Anne Goodchild, Betty Hancock,?, ?, ?, Joy Burling, ?; front row: Thelma Ellis, ?, Pam Jennings, Joan Burling, ?, Rita Jacobs.   (G)

Plate 64. Girl Guide group outside St. Mary's Church.   (G)

The scout troop which was begun by Mr Albert F. Gathercole also eventually met here with my father and his brother as leaders. The troop began in 1922 when they met in a barn at the rear of Sadler's shop in North Street, having six members, and its first leader when it registered in 1923 was the Curate . Uniforms in those days cost one pound and the boys bought them for fourteen shillings. Subscriptions were twopence per week. After fifty years the Scout troop's own building was opened in Hawthorn Way on 9th June 1973. For many years camps were held at Heacham at a cost of twenty five shillings (£1.25 new pence) a week including the rail fare.

Plate 65. Thought to be a committee in 1920?

Behind the Guildhall in Spring Close, is the site of the old castle and easily my favourite spot. The house at number 1 was once the home of a carpenter and undertaker. When I was a child there were more fields leading from the close and along the country lanes. Sadly some have been built on. I spent many hours wandering around completely alone, and in season I gathered armfuls of flowers such as wild violets, ox-eye daises, cornflowers, cowslips, buttercups and cuckoo pint, some of which were used to decorate the church at its various festivals and others would end up in jam-jars at home.

Amongst the hedgerows there would be sloes, blackberries, hips and haws and hops to collect. After a windy day there would always be firewood to gather, a very useful commodity in those days for either the old kitchen range or open fire. From these paths and fields I could wander to Hall Farm where my friend lived, or as far as North Street without going near the main road. One memorable day when I had my young cousin and sister with me we had just crossed one of these fields and were moving down the lane to the next one when the horses, no doubt disturbed by the flies and heat decided to give chase. Both my charges started to cry as the horses thundered towards us with their tails flying. I half carried and half pulled my cousin along and as there was no time to climb over the style we scrambled under the gate, my sister first, then my cousin, and just as I began to crawl under myself I could feel the warm breath of the horses down my back. What a relief it was to get into the next field, indifferent to the mud through which we squelched. I well remember too the time when the mound in the Spring Close was used for motor cycle scrambling where the course was reckoned to be quite a good one. On one occasion I thought I was marooned on the mound because of the bog but eventually I managed to find a way across it.

Plate 66. Lane beside the Spring Close.

BURWELL CASTLE AS IT PROBABLY WAS IN 1145

Plate 67. Drawing of the castle taken from Charles Lucas' book, the Fenman's World.

Plate 68. Last of the castle ruins.

Plate 69. Excavating at the castle site, Dr Palmer and Dr Lucas.
Courtesy Cambridge Antiquarian Society

Plate 70. Excavating at the castle site.   Courtesy Cambridge Antiquarian Society

Plate 71. Motor cycle scrambling in the Spring Close in the 1950s.   (G)

Back in 1935 during excavations on the castle site, the remains of a Roman settlement were discovered as well as relics of twelfth century pottery. The site could previously have been the site of an Anglo-Saxon fort. Fragments of coloured glass found at the same time were thought to have come from a private chapel at the Manor of the Abbot of Ramsey which he had requested that the Bishop of Ely should consecrate in 1246. They were red, green and blue in colour.

A once famous soldier named Mandeville was given estates in Oxford, Suffolk, Northants, Warwickshire, Berkshire, Essex, Cambridgeshire, Hertfordshire and Middlesex. He was also made constable of the tower of London. Geoffrey de Mandeville, his grandson, Earl of Essex invaded King Stephen's land and its religious houses, marched into the fens and seized the Isle of Ely. To defend the area from Mandeville, the King ordered castles to be built along the edges of the fens. One of these sites is in Spring Close nearby the spring and stream where the castle was built in the 1100s. It is probable that the moat was never filled with water as the castle was never finished. In August 1144 after capturing the castle, Geoffrey was riding round it when an archer in the castle wounded him in the head with an arrow. At first it only seemed like a slight wound but he was taken to Mildenhall where before he died in September, he asked his son to restore Ramsey Abbey. He was refused a Christian burial but some Templars took his body to London. The last remaining pieces of clunch wall of the castle rising to about eight feet were used by firemen to test their hoses and soon afterwards during a church service in about 1935 it collapsed with a great noise, causing considerable alarm to the cottages nearby.

Was it here, I wonder, where the Peace Festival was held in August 1814 on the Prince Regent's birthday? The day was ushered in by a discharge of canon and followed by the ringing of the church bells, many peals being rung. Ten dining tables were tastfully arranged with boughs and flowers, and an excellent band played in their midst. About a quarter before 2 o'clock the tables began to groan beneath the weight of hot plum puddings and roast and boiled beef of the very best quality. At 2 o'clock eight hundred persons sat down to partake of them. The first bugle announced grace which was said by the president at each table. Plenty of strong ale was provided and upon the removal of the cloths, there were pipes and tobacco. The sports which followed consisted of donkey-racing and jingling matches, and in the evening a dance was given for respectable inhabitants and their families all especially dressed up for an occasion upon which the 'beaux and belles were tripping on the light fantastic toe', till dawn the following day. The next evening the surplus ale was distributed. Rustic sports followed. On the Monday evening about five hundred women were regaled with tea and bread and butter.

As already stated Sunday School treats were held here and in July 1860 this was combined with a cottage garden exhibition of wild and garden flowers and vegetables for which prizes were awarded. The tent in which it was held was loaned by Dr Lucas.

Another such event was recorded on 19th July 1872. It seems that the schools up to this time had had individual treats, but on this particular day they were combined with the Parish Flower Show, which it is now called, for which there were three hundred entries. Five hundred children had tea and each received a toy or useful article. Seven hundred others had tea at a cost of sixpence each, in tents but they ran out of tickets. Wicken Band played and altogether three thousand people came. Several fine balloons went up and there were fireworks. An address was given by the Vicar (what a wonderful opportunity for him).

Plate 73. Pump in High Street.

Plate 72. Pump on Stock's Hill, 1990.
Mr John Richardson

In the 1970s Spring Close was surrounded by barbed wire to keep people out. It was privately owned until 1983 when it was bought by the Parish Council for twenty thousand pounds to be used for the benefit of the local people. The lane between the Spring Close and the Guildhall is called Mandeville.

Returning to the High Street and walking along on the left, we reach number 25 High Street which when I knew it, was Archie Hawkes' grocery shop but now sells antiques. Stock's Hill on the right, remains and still houses the one old water pump, one of several, others were at Swaffham Road, the Causeway, North Street and the Broads prior to the mains supply being laid in 1939.

Plate 74. View of the High Street from St. Mary's church tower   (G)

Across the road stands the old St. Mary's Church Parochial Junior school and the School House, on or near the site of the old St. Andrew's church. The school house was once occupied by the headmaster/mistress but when my father died it was not needed and it was let to my mother. We moved there during September 1936 and this was where I was to spend the next twenty years, although my mother stayed on until 1977. The premises had been built to house a girls' school in 1860 during the Rev. Cockshott's time at a cost of eight hundred pounds and was run by a headmistress and assisted by pupil teachers who received their own instruction at 7 o'clock in the morning even during the bad winter weather. The foundation stone was laid on 7th April, 1859 to cheers and peals of church bells. As in the boys' school, religious instruction was given daily by the vicar and the day would open and close with prayer. At church festivals the pupils would attend church services instead of receiving religious instruction in school. Although there was an annual government grant to make ends meet the children paid a small charge. Sometimes two girls would be sent round the village to sell their needlework. On one occasion they returned with seventeen pounds and fourpence, quite a considerable sum in those days. In October 1891 the school came under the Education Act.

Plate 75. St. Mary's School and School House, in the 1930s.

During the harvest, girls would be away gleaning or, in the spring helping their mothers with spring cleaning. Attendance also fell during outbreaks of scarlet fever, water-pox, smallpox, diphtheria, mumps, heavy colds and sore throats, winter snowstorms and severe thunderstorms in the summer. In 1880 the school was closed for fourteen weeks during an outbreak of fever when there were fourteen cases in five families. Occasionally on the recommendation of the Medical Officer the cane was administered for using bad language or putting out one's tongue, and on one occasion, because they had been inattentive the whole class had to march around the playground instead of playing. One school treat was to the Devil's Ditch when the vicar gave a prize for the best bunch of wild flowers. In 1867, three hundred children took part in a school festival by singing hymns during a procession. They listened to a sermon and partook of bran pie.

Plate 76. St. Mary's Schoolchildren, 1900.

I did not particularly enjoy my time spent at this school. I was frequently being told that I would never pass the 11+ which gave me little incentive to try, so it was not surprising that I failed miserably. Neither did I like being classed as delicate which meant lining up with two or three other pupils to receive my daily dose of a dessertspoonful of cod liver oil and malt. Before marching into school we children would line up in classes in the little back playground where our kitchen door was located. Mostly we played in the playground at the front of the school and house. Until the Second World War this gently sloped down to the front wall but when the soldiers were billetted there they made a dug-out near the wall and from then on it was rather uneven. Some of the soldiers were at first billeted with us but later we had evacuee families from Dover, Kent and London.

Plate 77. St. Mary's decorated cart, lady in crinoline could be Miss Johnson.   (G)

When piped water was installed at School House in about 1952, many bones were dug up from the garden and the school playground, including skulls and jaws with complete sets of teeth. Under our kitchen floor skeletons of babies were found. A complete adult skeleton was dug up from the playground and I believe was taken to the Archaeology department in Cambridge. Some waste land at the back of the school later housed a canteen and provided a new playground. This was where my sister and I played marbles, whip and top, bat and ball and rode our bicycles during our free time. After the new schools were built further down the village this school was leased to the Cambridgeshire Auxiliary Forces and when my mother moved, the house was leased to them also for about seven years. These buildings are now listed buildings and have been sold and the land at the back built upon.

Plate 78. St. Mary's School May day celebrations, 1925.   (G)

Plate 79. St. Mary's schoolchildren going for lunch in the Guildhall, 1938?   (G)

In the kitchen of our house was a bricked up doorway which would obviously have been used by the residing head to gain access to the school. It was a large, clunch built house, with four bedrooms as well as a small boxroom, a large kitchen, a back sitting room, large hall and large front sitting room. With walls eighteen inches thick, in summer it proved particularly cool. For a long time we had a range in the back sitting room which backed onto a small fire in the kitchen to heat the copper while in the front room was an open tiled fireplace. Many a time I have stood outside to watch for the sweep's brush to rise from out of the chimney pot, informing the sweep when it appeared. In the back garden was an old water pump which continued to be usable for a number of years. There was no bathroom or flush toilets for some time and ours, although in our garden and separated by a brick wall, was in a line with the school ones which were buckets over which were wooden seats with a trap door at the back for emptying. Mostly a man came and emptied them once a week. Steep steps led up from Mill Lane to the side of the house.

Plate 80. Class of St. Mary's schoolchildren in 1949; back row: Roy Marsh, John Brown, Michael Alecock, ?, Charlie Phelps; next row: Anne Horton, Mary Hanton, Hilary Nockles, Judith Sowerby, Brenda Carter, Delphine Fuller, Clive Collins, Jennifer Hammond, Wendy Barton; next row: Valerie Thompson, Derek Oliver, Brenda Bagstaff, Pat Day, ?, ?, John Hawkins, Reginald Fuller, Jennifer King; front row: Elaine Bagstaff, Margaret Pearman, Gillian Fuller, Mavis Fletcher.
Courtesy Miss Brenda Carter

Plate 81. Fancy dress Victory celebrations, taken outside St. Mary's School and School House, back row left to right: John Fuller, Dorothy Collins, Pam Glendon, Pat Johnson, Dorothy LePla, Tony Lack, Michael Beer, Margaret Bowen, ?, Daphne Carter, Shirley Mansfield, David Bailey; far left: Anne Goodchild; far right: Donald Boud; middle row: Terry Coombs, Marie Adams, Patrick Faircliffe, Heather Johnson, Maureen Willis, Alan Taylor, Pauline Housden, Barbara Barton, Robina Hawkins, ?, Kenneth Hawes, Jennifer Faircliffe; front row: Eileen Adams, Pauline Norton, Gillian Lack, Elaine Branch, Peter Blanchflower, Brian Sangster, Parr, Felicity Barton. Heather M. Richardson

In Mill Lane stands the only existing windmill, now restored by the Burwell Windmill Trust. The Mill is over one hundred and sixty years old and still retains all of the original machinery and its clunch built tower. It was last worked in 1955 and it must have been while it was still working that I was once allowed to visit it. It is known as Steven's Mill and the only one of four left in the village. It has a new cap and fantail, new sails and where necessary new or repaired floors. The wheat, known as Old Kent Longred produced flour of exceptional quality for which Burwell was justly famous.

Further along the High Street, at number 27, was a butcher's and a little further still is a small room from where we used to fetch our fish and chips supplied by Harry Reeve and his wife, the fishmonger and fish fryer. Their business was started by his mother

Plate 82. Windmill and 'new' bungalow. (G)

Plate 83. Archie Hawkes' shop and cottage, 1920s.

75

Plate 84. The High Street, 1920s. Courtesy Mrs F. Horton

Plate 85. The High Street 1920s. Courtesy Mrs F. Horton

Plate 86. Miss Ellis' Barber's shop at the White Horse.

Plate 87. The White Horse showing the entrance to the Bowls Club. (G)

Plate 88. Miss Beard, projectionist for film shows.   (G)

in a corrugated shed in the garden of their home in Mandeville. Orders which included fruit and vegetables were first delivered on a handcart and then by pony and trap. Originally the room had been the club room of the White Horse Hotel. Now it is demolished and replaced by a hairdressers. At the back of what was once the White Horse Inn, there was a Variety Hall named 'Rialto'. Travelling shows used it, and a cinema group, although they met opposition from the Gardiner Memorial Hall. This was also used for films (silent ones) run by Kirby and Mark. Their pianist was Mr Jack Fulcher, understudied by Mr Kelly Webb, the St. Mary's Schoolmaster. Later local residents took over the group at the Hall and took films to other villages. These films were shown by Mr

Ralph Wolsey, Miss E. Beard (who was a neighbour of our's) while Miss Ruby Lane acted as the pianist.

Plate 89. Group setting out for Newmarket races in fancy dress posing outside the Five Bells.

The White Horse was built in 1849 and in December was heralded in by a party, the tea being handsomely provided by Mrs C. Hunt, and the evening entertainment provided by the Newmarket and Burwell brass bands. In April 1851 the brothers and friends of the Odd Fellows Society met in the White Horse to celebrate their first anniversary. Before this dinner they enlivened the village by passing through in their usual costume, with flags and banners and accompanied by the Burwell Band. Dinner was served by Mr Carter in his customary liberal manner after which followed the general, loyal and other toasts. Many good songs were sung and the company dispersed at a late hour after having spent a very pleasant day. In June 1908, the Swimming Club held their first annual dinner and smoking concert in there. They were provided by the landlord, Mr Flint with roast beef, mutton, Yorkshire pudding, jellies, baked apples, custard, cheese and celery. The White Horse closed as an hotel in 1975.

Opposite the White Horse stands another Public House, the Five Bells built in the eighteenth century. A little further along is the Gardiner Memorial Hall, named after John Gardiner who left money for it to be erected. The foundation stone was laid by his sister-in-law Mrs Mary Anne Gardiner and the commemoration stone reads: 'Erected for the use of the inhabitants in accordance with the Will of the late Mr John Gardiner of this Parish'. He also left some money to be invested for the general benefit of the poor. When piped water and sewerage were to be brought to Burwell this hall was packed with people opposed to the idea. Between the wars Mr Harry Peachey an Independent and Parish representative campaigned for Burwell to have piped water but many people led by Mr Game and including Mr McBeath the chemist opposed the idea and won their case. However after the Second World War the Burwell people wanted to be connected to the sewer and of course they needed piped water for it by which time of course costs had risen. Despite the conflict between the two men, when at a later date Mr Game was dying, Mr Peachey, a staunch Methodist visited him. To those somewhat surprised who questioned him about this he replied that it was the Christian thing to do.

Plate 90. The High Street.   Courtesy Cambridge County Record Office

Plate 91. Dr Charles Lucas seated, with his family. (G)

Plate 92. The High Street.　　Courtesy Miss F. Horton

Plate 93. Bedlam Square. The occupants of these cottages shared a pump, water closet and bakehouse.

Plate 94. The Old Hall.   Courtesy Cambridge Antiquarian Society

Plate 95. Hon. Alexandrina Peckover opening the Congregational Sunday School, October 24th 1907.

Plate 96. Congregational Sunday School, 1907.

Plate 97. Congregational Sunday School about 1950.　　　Courtesy Mrs F. Horton

Plate 98. Congregational Chapel.

Plate 99. Rev. R.C. Jude, Congregational Minister in the 1930s.

Plate 100. The High Streeet, 1914.

The Burwell Choral Society of which I was a member gave concerts here and it has been the scene of many other concerts, housed fêtes in wet weather, exhibitions, meetings and dances, and was where I first learnt to do old time dancing. During the war soldiers were billeted here, and some of them were sent here to convalesce from a skin complaint. I understand that in 1916 it was insured against damage by aircraft.

Back on the other side of the road stands a house now occupied by Ellwood's the butcher, but where once lived Dr Charles Lucas, the author of 'The Fenman's World'. I knew it as Mark Smith's the butchers, where during the Second World War Mr Smith would kill a pig around Christmas time allowing regular customers to purchase half a pound of pork sausages for each member of the family. A luxury indeed! Dr Lucas' sisters, one of whom was once the church organist lived in a house opposite here, possibly at 'Tiptofts', the name deriving from the baronial family of Tibetot who probably possessed it as early as 1227.

I can still remember the last two almshouses next to the butchers but only because one day near here, my sister and I were happily skipping hand in hand when she tripped and fell knocking herself unconscious. One of the old ladies came out of her almshouse and took her in while I ran back and fetched my mother. The rent for the occupiers of these houses was one penny a year, and there were about fourteen almshouses in the village. The first lane on the left was one of several I used to frequent and which led down to the meadows. Beside it is Ramsey Manor and the other side of it used to stand Claydon's shop run by two sisters, Bertha and Ada Claydon, which sold practically everything from candles to sweets and haberdashery and also ran a local library service. The next lane, Hall Lane ran down between a house, which used to be the Manse for the Congregational Church Minister, and what I remember as Roy's shop, formerly a tailors, and then Vassiere's, the first part of which sold furniture and the other part was a general store. In 1932 my mother bought a carpet when it belonged to Hugh Taylor. It measured twelve by twelve feet, cost five guineas and lasted until 1975. Opposite this at number 68 was another butcher's shop, and either near Bedlam Square or attached to the Crown public house was a small building used by a cobbler, Nelson Drake. Here I would bring shoes to be mended by the 'snob'. I was never in a hurry to leave and was fascinated by the array of tools and the smell of leather and polish.

Hall Lane leads to Hall Farm, a late sixteenth century Tudor house, once a moated grange. In the early 1900s when part of the house was pulled down a long perpendicular window was revealed about sixteen or eighteen feet high, probably the west window of a chapel or banqueting hall. As St. John's priory stood across the adjoining meadow it was possible that this was part of the monastic ruin. A family of Johnsons lived at the Hall for several generations and took a very prominent part in all local and public affairs. An extensive fire in 1843 destroyed a large barn, a capacious stable, a cow-house, a quantity of barley in a barn, two stacks of wheat, two stacks of barley and two of oats, the whole of which was fortunately insured. All livestock except two and the dwelling house were saved by the efforts of the Burwell and Swaffham Prior fire engines. The high wind sent flakes of fire a quarter of a mile away and set fire to the thatched roof of the post office and nothing but the walls remained. A Thomas Bradley was convicted for setting fire to the premises and was sent to Parkhurst Prison, Isle of Wight for fifteen years. The next building along the High Street, now known as Trinity Church, was built in 1907 as the Congregational Church Sunday School, although it had many other uses. The Congregational church opposite has now been sold to the Tuckey Ford Organisation and has reverted to its original name of the Meeting House. The earliest burial recorded here was that of Robert Simondson on 13th July 1792. In November 1862 an event is recorded of two hundred people partaking of tea to commemorate the one hundred and fifteenth Anniversary of 'High Town Chapel'.

The church was formed on 9th June 1692 and consisted of sixteen members who came from six parishes. By 1707 its membership had grown to one hundred and thirty six drawn from twenty two villages. The meeting house built in 1798 had a gallery all the way round it. Mr John Taylor the tanner contributed seven hundred pounds towards it. After tea many others were admitted to a public meeting where Pastor J. Hicks gave a brief history of the Independent cause in this town. There were several addresses and at 7 p.m.. the Rev. George Hitchon of Brandon preached an eloquent sermon on the text: Zecharia 4:11-2. Several pieces of sacred music were sung during tea by the Burwell choir. The year before that, there is a record of the death of Robert Casburn, farmer and clerk and manager to the

Member of Paliament Mr E. Ball. Mr Casburn was well known for miles around as a local preacher, connected with the Independents, a man of proverbial uprightness, integrity and amiability. He was devoted to the cause of religion and the diffusion of popular education. His heart was ever alive to missionary enterprises, and being ever alive to God and the benefit of his fellow creatures so far as his means and abilities allowed. He was a living example of what a Christian should be. Heavy rain prevented one hundred schoolchildren from singing a hymn at his graveside as intended, but they lined the approaches to a thronged Chapel. A few months previously he had been presented with a richly bound Bible and a gold pencil case by his Reach friends. Rev. Hicks officiated at the funeral assisted by Rev. Mathers from Soham. A funeral sermon was preached the following day by Rev. Hicks on the text from Acts 22:16, 'And now why tarriest thou? arise and be baptized, and wash away thy sins, calling on the name of the Lord'. After a fire in 1861 the chapel was rebuilt in 1866, and later it was known as the Congregational church.

Plate 101. Mrs Warren with her daughter Barbara outside 'Droford' in 1933. Courtesy Mrs Barbara Hayward, the girl in the picture

Plate 102. Mr MacBeath the chemist. (G)

Plate 103. Mr MacBeath's shop sign. (G)

Plate 104. The interior of Mr MacBeath's chemist shop, 1925.

In November 1901 shortly after the evening service smoke was seen coming from the roof near the chimney. The alarm was given when it was realized that part of the building was on fire. The villagers gave prompt assistance and the village fire engine was speedily brought to the spot and the fire brigade soon put out the fire, but not before a certain amount of damage was done to the building. In 1972 it became the United Reformed church which was commemorated with a service of thanksgiving with others on 15th October in Great St. Mary's Church. In 1988 the congregation united with the Methodists, and as mentioned above is now the Trinity Church.

On the site of the present pharmacy there once stood the Droford Mineral Water Works owned by the Rickard family. Mr Rickard, from Brixton, London, started making lemonade here in 1890. Originally the bottles had screw stoppers but later the glass ball seal came into use. During the 1914/18 war, troops living in tents on Mid-summer Common Cambridge had two cart-loads of lemonade delivered to them daily. Some of the produce went by barge to Reach and Upware and at Christmas time ginger wine and raisin wine was made. Following the departure of one or two managers, his daughter was put in charge of production while Mr W. Guyatt was manager, he had the option to buy but decided to branch out on his own and started a business in North Street. Mr LePla carried on the business but when it closed in 1915, he went into farming, becoming the first man in Burwell to grow sugar beet. Mr Guyatt carried on his business on the Causeway followed by his son William who decided in 1974 at the age of eighty years to close it down. In 1933 a tailor Mr E. Warren moved with his family into the old house at Droford. Neither building now exists. An earlier pharmacy once stood on the site of the present Spar grocers but in about 1919 Benjamin Morley, the chemist was found hanged. Another chemist, Mr MacBeath still dispensed medicine at the age of ninety years. The pathway between here and the bank is still known as Cuckold's Row and it was somewhere near here that the tragic barn fire took place. This may have been the shoemakers row which once existed in the High Street and where a house was destroyed by fire in 1671.

Still in the High Street on the right is the other entrance to Mill Lane or the 'backway', and past this the Crown Public House.

Plate 105. The Mansfield family with some of their vehicles outside their premises in 1926. Courtesy Mr Jim Neale

91

Plate 106. Burwell bus built in 1931. Courtesy Mr Jim Neale

Plate 107. Burwell bus built in 1937. Courtesy Mr Jim Neale

Plate 108. June 9th 1979. Courtesy Mr Jim Neale

Plate 109. June 9th 1979. Courtesy Mr Jim Neale

93

Plate 110. Reconditioned bus at a recent carnival in 1990
Heather M. Richardson

Plate 111. Parsonage Farm.   Courtesy Cambridge Antiquarian Society

Opposite here once stood the garages and offices of the Burwell and District Motor Company owned by the Mansfield family. The business was started on the Causeway by George Mansfield who had a cobblers and bicycle repair shop. When he acquired a motor-cycle and side-car he found it useful for fetching a bank clerk from Newmarket to Burwell once a week and finding there was a need for transport, he bought a taxi and then a larger one. The business flourished and he bought a purpose built twenty six seater bus in 1924. Number 1 ran from the village to Cambridge and as the business developed other local villages were incorporated and excursions ran to Yarmouth and Felixstowe. When he died in 1935 his widow took the driving seat and was assisted by her two sons and daughters. By 1979 Horrie and his two sisters found it increasingly difficult to carry on and it was decided to allow a takeover. And so on 9th June four brown and cream buses made their final run to Cambridge, one of the drivers being Jim Neale, who like his father before him had been one of the company's employees. Special commemorative tickets printed on cream or brown card were issued with the words 'Burwell and District Motor Service—1921-1979— Souvenir Ticket issued on last day of operation June 9th 1979', and had a print of a pair of Burwell vehicles on the reverse side. They were in great demand by collectors and enthusiasts. A lot of the villagers were waiting at the garage to see the buses return with headlights blazing and horns blaring. When I travelled backwards and forwards to Cambridge in the early 1950s a weekly ticket would cost seven shillings and sixpence out of my weekly pay of two pounds, twelve shillings and sixpence. Jim Neale is the founder member of the Burwell & District Bus Preservation Society, and in 1982 he bought a single decker and spent the next five years repairing it, the money being raised by collecting scrap for recycling. The bus has won a number of awards at rallies. Not only were Jim and his father Mansfield's employees, but Jim's uncle worked for them as a conductor. It is gratifying to know that the bus company will not be forgotten.

Down the side of these premises, part of which is now being used by an Insurance company, is Parsonage Lane which leads to Parsonage Farm. This was once the site of the Priory of St. John and belonged to Ramsey Abbey. Up until about a hundred years ago it was the Parsonage until the Vicarage was built in the High Street. Parts of it are medieval but the main part of the house was built about 1600. At one time part of it was used as a malting house, one of nine in the village and once housed a profitable industry. It was also used as a slaughter house. Edward Ball, an MP for Cambridgeshire was once a tenant although he lived at Burwell House.

Plate 112. Cottages in Low Road.   Courtesy Cambridge Antiquarian Society

    Another tenant in the mid eighteenth century was Salisbury Dunn who lived in the Manor House. He was a wealthy man and proud of his possessions. He remarked to his friends that 'one day the big bell will toll and people will say, "Dear me, there passes a man worth one hundred thousand pounds."' At his death his three sons and seven daughters each received ten thousand pounds. In 1924 the County Council bought the property and let it out to smallholders. It is now owned by a commune who have restored much of it and have created employment for themselves and others.

    Tunbridge Farm was a moated grange and was separated from Parsonage Farm by a water course which formed part of the moat. The house was built out of a portion of the old Priory and was later separated into two buildings. At one time it also had a secret chamber. Despite yearly replanting a Cherry orchard near here which once produced beautiful fruit in abundance,   ceased to flourish when the water-level of the fen was lowered by two feet. In prosperous times anyone might by the payment of sixpence eat cherries to his heart's content all day long.

Plate 113. Number 10 Low Road.

Parsonage Lane continues into Low Road and along here at the 'Poplars' a printer had a small business from about 1890-1920. He did the work himself and would print large bills about sales of land, cattle and farm equipment as well as letterheads and billheads for the local traders. His brother married Miss Rickard from the mineral works. This may also have been the house where lived a Nathan Ball, gentleman of culture and substance. His son Fitz-Ball became famous as the writer of the song 'My Pretty Jane', and I recount the story as follows from the Strand Magazine (June 1903).

'When Sir Henry Bishop wrote the music of "My Pretty Jane," so dissatisfied was he with his work that he consigned it to the waste-paper basket. It happened that the manager of Vauxhall Gardens wanted a new song, so with Edward Fitz-Ball, who wrote the words of "My Pretty Jane", he called on Sir Henry Bishop to see what could be done.

Plate 115. Miss Jennings who lived near the Pound Hill. She kept a boarding house for theatrical stars before retiring to Burwell where she then became famous for her fortune telling at fêtes and shows. She died at the age of 97. (G)

Plate 114. Mary Sharp's gravestone in St. Mary's Churchyard.   Mr John Richardson

Sir Henry Bishop was not at home, but on wandering about the room Edward Fitz-Ball caught sight of a piece of manuscript paper in the waste-paper basket. Snatching the music paper from the receptacle, Fitz-Ball found that it contained his song "My Pretty Jane". Without waiting for the composer's return, the pair of depredators went off with the song, which was sung the same evening by one of the principal tenors of the day, and received with rapturous applause.

Thus by a lucky accident was preserved the song which for so many years was one of the great successes of Sims Reeves. Like "The Lass of Richmond Hill", "Robin Adair", etc., "My Pretty Jane" was a real person. When Edward Fitz-Ball was a young man he lived in a small village (Burwell) in Cambridgeshire, and in one of the lanes along which the young man frequently passed lived a very pretty girl called Jane. She was the daughter of a farmer, and from her window she would occasionally smile and nod to young Fitz-Ball as he passed by. On one summer's day the budding author sat on a stile near the farmer's house, and in a few minutes wrote the words of the pleasing song. Probably the "bloom was on the rye" in the field hard by where the youthful poet sat. Whether "Pretty Jane" ever responded to the invitation to meet the author "in the evening" we know not; there is some reason to think she may have done so, as there was in existence a portrait of the lady painted in oils by Fitz-Ball'. It is reputed to have hung over the mantelpiece in the panelled room of Nathan Ball's house. Fitz-ball attributed his creative abilities and vivid imagination to the romantic village of Burwell and the beautiful countryside that surrounded it where he spent his childhood, he was educated in Newmarket'.

At the east end of the parish church a gravestone is erected to the memory of Mary Sharp. It bears the following inscription:

> In memory of Mary Sharp, aged 38.
> Come all my friends who see me die, for I am brokenhearted;
> Not a wish had I to live, since from my love I parted.
> When I am laid in my cold grave, and should it be to-morrow,
> Write on my stone here lies a maid who drank a cup of sorrow.

There is a well-grounded tradition in the village that Mary Sharp was the veritable 'Pretty Jane' of Fitz-Ball's memorable song, and that she died of a broken heart. One of the old barns in Low Road was used to store food during the Second World War.

Plate 116. Shops on Pound Hill in 1924. (G)

Plate 117. Granny Doe and her husband with their stall outside their shop on Pound Hill at Burwell Feast in 1926. (G)

Plate 118. Skeleton from Saxon Cemetery. (G)

Plate 119. Excavating at the site of the Saxon Cemetery. (G)

101

Plate 121. Victoria lime pits in 1900 at the back of the Crown Public House.

Plate 120. Bronze workbox found in the Saxon Cemetery

Plate 123. Memorial cottage, 1921. Courtesy Miss Winnifred Peachey

Plate 122. Mr Heeks, the miller outside the Mill on Newmarket Road.

Back on the main road is the Pound Hill where years ago stray cattle would be kept until collected by their owners on payment of a fine. The first house, which boasts two inglenook fireplaces is now open as Inglenook Crafts and Snacks which I would think is very welcomed in Burwell.

The house which is now the postmaster's residence once belonged to Granny Doe and her husband. He had a sadler's shop while next door she sold sweets. Burwell Feast was held annually at Whitsun with stalls and 'shies' on Pound Hill and the larger items at the back of the White Horse. The Sadler's shop would be cleared and Granny Doe who normally sold comics, sweets and toys would sell stewed prunes on saucers, five for a halfpenny, ten a penny. On one occasion she sold as many as five stone (70 pounds). Sweets were bought for as little as one farthing. Grandfather Doe made seed wart cure and sold it at one shilling a bottle. On the Sunday following the feast the Church parade would take place. In 1851 one report states that the village had been very gay during the feast week. Large numbers of persons of all sects from the neighbourhood had been attracted by the different amusements on offer. A ball was held on the Monday evening under the management of the Independent Order of Oddfellows which was well and respectably attended. No expense was spared by the host of the White Horse Inn in fitting up his house for the comfort and convenience of his friends. On the Wednesday a party of about four hundred persons had a pleasure excursion on the water, after which a supper was served up by host Danby of the Fox Inn.

In 1868 there were gingerbread stalls, swingboats and an Australian acrobat. People danced in the inns until a late hour. A prize of one shilling was given to anyone who was insane enough to eat 'half a pint of bran'; a quarter of a pound of tobacco was offered as a prize for a 'smoking match', there was a race for a new bonnet, and the challenge of a slimy pole for a new hat. Doe's premises were used later to start a cycle shop, with a sweet shop attached. My mother tells me how my father once owned a motorcycle, which he drove one day over the green and straight through one of the shop windows. The next day when he was out, his mother sold the motorcycle.

Between 1808-1853, Mike Bailey, a colourful character flourished. Every morning the vicar, 'Parson Baines' would go to his house to check up on the latest news. No doubt this gave him the title of 'Parson Baines' factotum. Mike Bailey also the postmaster and a sort of town clerk, wrote a good hand and as very few people could write he did all the correspondence of the village. In a small house on Pound Hill he kept one of several existing small schools. Parish records show that poor children were being taught at a charity school from at least 1743.

Plate 124. Liberals association at Berkley House.
Courtesy Miss Winnifred Peachey

On the opposite side of the road, off the Burwell-Exning road and the main street and just behind the Red House, lay the old Victoria Lime Pits. From 1884 and in the immediate following years about fourteen skeletons were found near here. But by 1924 no trace of them could be found. From 1924-29 excavations were carried out under the direction of T.C. Lethbridge on adjoining land belonging to Dr Lucas, where 125 graves were carefully examined. Most of them seemed to have been buried with their heads to the West in the Christian style and had with them iron knives and other associated articles which have mostly been lost. Some had obviously met with a violent death, one having probably been decapitated. Another was probably devoured by wolves or were the remains of a gibbetted body. Most of the bodies had been fully clothed with traces of leather belts with buckles where the knives were carried. Bone combs were found with some of the women and sometimes work boxes. Wooden boxes containing trinkets, such as Indian cowrie shells were sometimes found, also such articles as toothpicks and spoons. Food was put with many of the bodies, including nuts and a drinking bowl.

Plate 125. Liberals association garden party at Berkley House on June 27th 1911. Courtesy Miss Winnifred Peachey

A pit nearby between eighteen to twenty feet in diameter and five feet six inches deep was also excavated. The floor contained fragments of Romano-British pottery, roof tiles, burnt stones, animal bones and traces of wood and charcoal. No Saxon pottery was found and occupation must have taken place either in the Roman period or very soon after, and is unlikely to be connected to the cemetery.

The Causeway, or 'causey', meaning a raised footpath, or 'monks' way', by which names it was once known is an avenue of elm trees which extended from Bunker's Hill (near the Saxon cemetery) to 'cross trees' which consisted of trees planted in the form of a cross situated in the vicinity of the Co-op, Hall's and Sadler's shops. It is reputed to have been made by the monks many hundreds of years before to shelter and protect people coming from the lower end of the village to church. A monks' cell in North Street was erected in about 1420 and it is probable that the causeway came into being then. The main street to North Street was not in existence until 1916, the oldest and main street having been up to this time Newnham Street which ran parallel to the Causeway.

Plate 126. Ness Road, 1934.

On the corner of the Causeway and Ness Road stands the King William the Fourth Public house built in 1830. It was built as an ale house and when an application was made for a spirits' licence it was turned down. The judges expressed the opinion that Burwell did not need gin shops such as existed in Piccadilly with an accompanying female population. Several applications finally gained approval. On the opposite corner of the Ness Road stood a house where I used to go to pay my mother's paper bill. Arthur Doe, who lived here and was known as Matey Doe used to meet the 7.00 a.m. train each morning with his trap and a donkey called Billy to collect the papers and smoked fish. He also sold delicious home made ice-cream.

Some of the older residents may well remember when Ness Road was just a dirt track where one could go blackberrying. The road was named after Henry de Ness, a henchman of William the Conqueror. After I left Burwell a junior school was opened in 1961 along this road but like the one in Parsonage Close, it has since been pulled down and the site also built upon. Between the Burwell and Fordham boundary there once stood a toll-gate. The cost to pass through was sixpence and the last toll was collected in December 1905.

Plate 127. Dedication of war memorial.

Somewhere near Breach Farm, a Robert Stephenson who lived in the Manor House built a cement works in the early 1900s. He employed about forty men on each of two shifts of twelve hours a day and in 1919, this changed to three eight hour shifts. The men had thirty minutes for meals. During the 1914/18 war some of the men were paid fourpence halfpenny per hour, some threepence halfpenny and boys handling fuel twopence halfpenny. The pit was eighty feet deep and the chalk was excavated with crowbars, shovels and barrows. Work ceased during the 1926/27 slump period.

Back to the Causeway just past the present Post Office at number 19 is a dwelling which was built as a home for a nurse and as a memorial to those who lost their lives in the First World War. It was officially opened on the 20th February, 1921 and the nurse paid a

Plate 128. Dedication of memorial extension 1952? (G)

Plate 129. War memorial, 1990. Mr John Richardson

Plate 130. Group of A.R.P.'s 1939-45.   Courtesy Mr & Mrs Eric Jacobs

Plate 131. Collecting the last toll on Ness Road, December 1905.

Plate 132. The Toll-gate from the Fordham side.
Courtesy Cambridge Antiquarian Society

Plate 133. Closing the Toll gate, December 1905. Courtesy Mrs F. Horton

Plate 134. Horse and trap.

Plate 135. The first car in Burwell.	Courtesy Cambridge County Records Office

Plate 136. Doe's ices in Ness Road, nicknamed 'Icicula bell'. One of Dr Elliott's children serving. (G)

Plate 137. Matey Doe, the last town crier with his donkey, Billy. (G)

113

Plate 138. British Legion on Armistice Day 1923 with Nurse Lillian Hodges. (G)

Plate 139. British Legion, 1956. Courtesy Mr & Mrs Eric Jacobs

114

Plate 140. The Pound Hill 1909.

Plate 141. The King William IVth Public House, 1925.   (G)

rent of five pounds per annum to the Trustees of the cottage. Her duties then consisted of attendance at childbirth and cases of sickness. With a population of about two thousand the nurse went about her duties on a bicycle which included visits to outlying Fen Farms. I well remember Nurse Bolton, a Queen's nurse who was here for forty four years. The names of the dead from both world wars are listed on the wall of this cottage as well as on the memorial in the church.

The Burwell Ex-Service Mens' and Social Club was originally housed in a wooden building before the present brick built one. The club was first formed in 1921 for the ex-servicemen of the village who had served in the first World War and was then called the Burwell Ex-Servicemens' Club and the building was called the 'Hut'. In 1923 its name was changed to the Burwell British Legion Club but all ties with the British Legion were broken in 1954. Nearby is the Police house, where P.C. Oliver was the incumbent during some of the time I lived in the village.

Plate 142. Guides and Brownies in the 1940s. Back row left to right: Joyce Fuller, Wendy Barnet, Elaine Branch ?, ?, ?; next row: Margaret Baker, ?, ?, Jackie Phelps, ?, ?, Violet Hills, Evelyn Nockles, ?, June Norton; next row: ?, Heather Crosby, ?, Wendy Barton, Judith Sowerby, Brenda Bagstaff, Elaine Bagstaff, Jennifer Ship; front row: ?, ?, Jill Fuller, Pam Collins, ?, ?, Maureen Lawrence, Kathleen Hubbard, ?, Marleen Collins, ? (G)

Number 25, was formerly the residence of the registrar of births and deaths. His office was converted to Doe's sweetshop and next door a cycle shop, a business which began in 1919 on the Pound Hill. My first bicycle was purchased from here and this was also where we brought our radio accumulators to be recharged. Number 27 was once the post office after it was moved from number 53. It was owned by two sisters by the name of Secrett, one of whom Miss Rhoda, was a cripple. Every Sunday her sister would tie her wheelchair to the back of her tricycle and then pedal away to the chapel at Swaffham Prior. The post office housed a little shop and it was not unknown when they were weighing biscuits for them to break one in half in order to weigh the exact quantity. After they died the premises became a cafe for a short while.

Number 33 the home of Mr Albert and Mrs Joan Gathercole, was a familiar house to me as this was where I went at the age of eight for my piano lessons. Their dog, Bonnie would lie under the piano and on occasions it was impossible not to kick the piano when the dog decided to make a move. Whilst waiting my turn for a lesson there was always a supply of Arthur Mee's childrens' newspapers to read. Albert was Works Manager of the Brickworks and the Chemical Works during his working life but had many other interests, including public duties as councillor, school governor, and trustee to various charities. He wrote a number of articles about the history of Burwell for Clunch magazine gathering his material from over sixty years of life in the village. He also wrote a guide to St. Mary's church, and he was associated with the Parish Church choir both as singer and choir master, as well as the Choral Society. At various times he acted as secretary and treasurer of the Parochial Church Council for many years. As previously stated, he founded the Burwell Scout troop in 1923 and at one time was chairman of the Newmarket Scouts Council. He also helped to administer some of the Burwell charities, in one case for as long as thirty years. The Gathercoles were a kindly couple, most hospitable to me and to many of my friends. Later when I stopped having piano lessons they took my friends and I on many trips to Cambridge to services at King's College Chapel on a Sunday followed by tea somewhere, either the Copper Kettle in King's Parade or in the summer to a cafe near Abingdon crossroads. During the evening, weather permitting we would often go for strolls along Fleam Dyke.

Plate 143. The Causeway, 1920. (G)

Plate 144. The Causeway. Courtesy Cambridge County Records Office

Plate 145 The cycle club, 1900s.

Plate 146. The Post Office on the Causeway.

Plate 147. The Causeway, 1900.

Plate 148. The Wesleyan Methodist Chapel copied from a photograph in a booklet commemorating its centenary in 1935.

Opposite number 33 lived a mutual friend of myself and the Gathercoles, Daphne Carter whose parents at that time had a fish and chip shop. This is now divided into three businesses, a greengrocer's, a betting shop and a ladies' hairdressers. At one time the premises were used as a fashionable dress shop run by Mr E. Kellaway and Miss G. Parr. Another time it was a cycle repair shop, perhaps the one owned by Mr H. Piches who had a cycle shop in 1906 and ran a thriving cycle club. His advertisement claimed that all his repairs were guaranteed.

Number 38 was once a ladies' hairdressers while next door was another cycle shop in one section and a confectioners in the other. Guyatt's mineral water works used to be at number 42. Number 46-48 was for many years a butcher's shop with another at 13 the Leys. Yet another butcher's shop belonging to the Co-op was run by Bert Norton and this is where the present Chinese take-away now operates. Mrs Hills, the mother of Violet another of my friends, tells me that during the Second World War the cellar was used by her and other neighbours as an air raid shelter.

On the right near the end of the Causeway stands what was once the Wesleyan Methodist Chapel, now a Grade II listed building of architectural interest and converted into work units and living accommodation. The land of twenty six perches for the first chapel was bought for thirty pounds and the chapel, a small square building and then known as the Wesleyan Methodist was opened in 1835. By 1862, seventy five per cent of its members requested that the then incumbent should resign but when he refused a request was made to the Burwell School to use its schoolroom. Permission was given and the minister eventually left. In the same year the revival at Reach was being talked about, inspired by a wonderful young man James Smith. This congregation wanted a revival so permission was given for James to preach at Burwell for three months. The school room was opened on April 7th 1862 and he took the services here with thirty eight members. During the nine months he was in the village before entering Spurgeon's College in January 1863 forty new converts were received into the church and the congregations were overflowing. Cottage prayer meetings were held as well as the usual Thursday evening service, which were well attended. It was the talk of the village and people sneered, despised and spoke ill of those attending. A song was composed and a man was paid to go through the village both to sing it and to sell copies of it. But the congregation ignored it and carried on with their meetings.

One, a John Peachey walking past jeering with a group of young men one Sabbath, said, 'There, if ever I am fool enough to go into that room, I hope they will carry me out on all fours'. The very same evening this same young man went into the schoolroom and sat amongst the congregation. While a new convert from Reach was praying earnestly for salvation to come to that room, there was a loud cry, a noise, and someone fell on the floor. It was the same John Peachey who had been smitten down by the Spirit and could not move. He was carried out on all fours by two individuals. He came back thanking God aloud that he had entered that room and that the Lord had answered his poor mother's prayers. He went home rejoicing that in Jesus, he was saved and his sins forgiven. He became an earnest Christian and married a young Christian woman, Jane Turner, a cook. She had been to the British Schoolroom and returned to her place of work. The housemaid perceiving her in an hysterical state called the owner of the house to come and help. When he asked her what was the matter she said, in tears, 'My sins, sir'. 'Oh', he said, 'you want the physician Jesus Christ for that. Let us kneel down and ask Jesus to save you'. As they knelt down, and she wept and prayed, the housemaid joined in. Then there was a knock at the door and the nursemaid came in. 'Please sir, I am as great a sinner as Jane Turner and Lettie, may I come in'? After praying all three rose up rejoicing in their salvation, their tears gone and their faces beaming with joy.

A Mr Jacob Wisbey of Cambridge baptised publicly those who wished in the river while the Rev J. Keed of Zion Baptist Chapel, Cambridge, baptised adults by immersion, *or* baptised infants, as the question of baptism was and still is a controversial subject. Others, young and old were converted. A public tea was held on January 1st, 1863. While it was usual to hold a New Years' meeting, this one was used publicly to thank God for allowing James Smith to come to Burwell and blessing him while here, to thank him for his labours and to wish him God speed. A collection of twelve pounds, ten shillings and sixpence was presented to him as a small tribute of gratitude and respect. There were two hundred and fifty people at the tea and four hundred and fifty at the public meeting. Mr Edward Ball the MP presented the purse and expressed the feelings of all the subscribers and friends.

Plate 149. Commemorative stones of British School and the Village College.
Mr John Richardson

Plate 150. Children of the British School about 1910. Back row left to right: Rose Jennings, Olive Palmby, Olive Flack, Marjory Norton, Nesta Burrows, Ivy Heffer; front row: Winnifred Peachey, Ivy Durrant, Miss Fitzpatrick (Headmistress), Alice Warren, Maud Fuller. Courtesy Miss Winnifred Peachey

Plate 151. Miss Fitzpatrick, a very strict Headmistress of the British School. Courtesy Miss Winnifred Peachey

In 1884 the chapel was enlarged by nine feet to become a rectangular building, the expenses being mostly met by legacies from a Miss Parr and Mr John Peachey, the convert mentioned above. It was enlarged again at a cost of three hundred and seventy three pounds with a stone laying ceremony on August 3rd, 1914 the day war broke out. In 1885 the Sunday School hymn books cost one penny or twopence each and Bibles, eightpence each. By 1924 it was requested that all should be free. The centenary was celebrated in 1935 with a decision to build a Sunday School room at a cost of around six hundred pounds. The foundation stone for this was laid at the rear of the chapel in July 1939 although almost as soon as it was built it was taken over by the army. The centenary services took place on Sunday June 30th at 11.00 a.m. and 6.30 p.m. and were conducted by Rev. W.T.A. Barber. At 2.15 p.m. a special young peoples' service was held and conducted by Mr Robert Ready of Wood Ditton, a former old scholar. The next day a sermon was preached at 4.00 p.m. by Rev. Colin A. Roberts followed by a tea at 5.30 p.m. and a public meeting at 7.00 p.m. Previous Sunday School anniversaries had been held in the British Schoolroom. Sadly this once well attended chapel would have needed forty thousand pounds spent on it for necessary repairs so it was sold in July 1988 for one hundred and twenty five thousand pounds for redevelopment, and the congregation united with the United Reformed church in the High Street calling themselves the Trinity Church.

Next door to the chapel once stood a house with a small shop attached which I remember well. At different times it sold fish, fruit, sweets and lastly fishing tackle, but when Mrs Hill had it as a sweet shop the school children could buy four sweets such as sherbet dabs for one penny.

The next building is the present village college. A Miss Sarah Ball, daughter of Edward Ball pressed her father as to the need for a public school and a public meeting was held on 28th May 1845. A barn was decorated and three hundred people paid fivepence a head to take tea which had been provided by well wishers. A building fund was launched with Edward Ball as chairman/treasurer, Rev D. Flower as secretary and eleven other committee members, their first duty being to raise funds. A Mr Joseph Kent of Swaffham offered the committee a piece of land for five pounds to give it a title and then donated the five pounds back. The foundation stone was dug from the grave of Sarah Ball who had died in October 1845 having suffered long ill-health. The stone was engraved with her name. The school with desks and other fittings was built at a cost of two hundred and eighty two pounds and eighty two pence and was duly opened on April 9th 1846 with one hundred and sixty children on the register. The first Head, a Miss Poulter was appointed at a salary of forty pounds a year.

A public tea was held in the barn mentioned earlier when one hundred and seventy people paid fivepence each. They went to the school room where a short service was held, after which they returned to the barn where addresses were given. On one of the first motto flags was written, in gold letters, 'The British School system has for its basis "The Word of God"'. The first child in each family was charged twopence a week and subsequent children one penny. In 1846 a school library was begun, the children having collected two pounds eight shillings and sevenpence. An appeal to the Religious Tract Society produced books to the value of five pounds despite the fact that only two pounds was sent to them. In October 1850 a burglar entered the school using false keys and took away the missionary box containing one pound five shillings destroying the childrens work in flannel and calico and leaving books strewn over the floor. A reward of three guineas was offered upon conviction of the offender. In 1862 a new classroom was added, connected to the older room by folding doors and the occasion celebrated with a tea and a public meeting. Two hundred people were expected but two hundred and fifty people arrived. Every seat was taken. At 7 o'clock it was densely crowded and every spot of standing room was used and many could not gain admission. An introductory address by Thomas T. Ball was given and the 'certificate of merit' pupils in the 'sol-fa' singing class in the village sang several select pieces. Rev. Holmes of Mildenhall gave the first address in an earnest, eloquent style, full of point and power which was most attentively listened to and much approved and applauded. An interesting and instructive speech was given by Rev. J. Keed of Cambridge and was rapturously received. The cost of the classroom, one hundred and seventeen pounds ten shillings, with previous donations and the collections on this day, was met by the end of the meeting. The school was now capable of holding four hundred pupils. In 1871 a new wall was erected and a new front gate added. Annual meetings with donated teas helped with school funds together with government grants, collections and donations. In 1877 the fees were increased to threepence for the first child and twopence for any subsequent children in the same family, although payments were not enforced if the family was poor. Several teachers were asked to resign when there were adverse reports from Her Majesty's Inspectors. Children received annual prizes and the teaching staff given books as an encouragement, and buns and oranges were distributed. The Jockey Club and Cambridge University were by now giving grants to the school.

In 1894 plans were approved to demolish the old cloak room and rebuild this across from where it had been. At the fortieth anniversary in 1886 heavy rain kept numbers down to one hundred and three people for tea. One hundred and fifty seven prizes were presented, ten of which were for attendance, and the rest for examination results. Books were also presented to teachers as a mark of the committee's satisfaction of efficiency during the year. A report

Plate 152. Teachers of the British School about 1918-20, back row: Gladys Fuller, Fanny Jennings, Winnie Lawrence, Annie Turner; front row: Ada Claydon, Miss Fitzpatrick (Headmistress), Eva Wilderspin, Ellen Claydon.
Courtesy Miss Winnifred Peachey

Plate 153. British School football team, 1936-37.

Plate 154. Secondary Modern School.

Plate 155. Secondary Modern School Speech day.   (G)

of 1895 was of overcrowding with no room for the children to march etc. The headteacher here in the late 1890s would administer punishment with a chairleg. The school had a fortnights holiday at Christmas and a week at Easter and Whitsun. The school would close if it was needed for flower shows, elections or comparable occasions there being no village hall at that time. Attendances were low in inclement weather or when there was outbreaks of water pox (a complaint caused by larvae of the hookworm entering the skin, and probably caught while bathing in stagnant water) influenza, mumps, chickenpox, ringworm, scarlet fever, impetigo of the face, and if the outbreak was severe enough the school would close.

On May 1st, 1902 the girls went May dolling. They decorated their dolls with flowers and placed them in shallow baskets covered with a cloth. If one wished to see the doll the cover would be removed and a payment made which was very useful pocket money. In 1904, one hundred and seventy three children who had not been absent or late were given small picture cards. If a child managed to collect ten of these cards they were exchanged for one larger illuminated card. Eight of these large cards at the end of the two years would procure a school attendance medal. In October 1906 a cookery class was started for eighteen girls. In 1911 two girls received watches for eight years' perfect attendance and one girl a Bible for three years. The next year one girl received a medal and a bar for nine years' perfect attendance. By now girls were being recommended for the Girls' County School in Cambridge and swimming lessons were begun for girls. By 1915 needlework and home nursing were taught and there is the first mention of a school dentist. Although the local Education Authority reported that discipline and behaviour were good, obviously the odd incidents arose.

During the 1914-18 war the children suggested that instead of their receiving prizes the money should go to St. Dunstan's and in 1917 on two afternoons the teachers were allowed to take some children blackberrying from the hedgerows, for the troops.

From January 1923 a number of changes took place and the school was classified as a senior school. Children under eleven years were transferred to St. Andrew's and St. Mary's with the older children from these schools and the boys' school transferring to the senior school. At this time the headmaster introduced woodwork for the boys. After Easter, children also came from Swaffham Prior and Reach (although there were times when they were disinclined to come) and a plot of land was secured for gardening for both boys and girls.

When I came to the school in 1945 it was known as the Secondary Modern School and we too did gardening and I remember beehives being kept on this piece of land. In April 1923 the school closed for the occasion of the wedding of the Duke of York and on May 1st the three schools closed and May day was celebrated in a field owned by Mr Stephenson. Three May Queens were crowned amidst the singing and Maypole dancing. In July one hundred and seven pupils were taken to Clacton, some never having been to the sea before. It was not unheard of for summer temperatures to reach seventy eight to ninety one degrees Fahrenheit and with those temperatures cookery and gardening classes would be suspended. In 1933 children suffered sunstroke and sick headaches. Brown paper covered the windows as there were no blinds. However in the winter the temperatures dropped to thirty three degrees Fahrenheit but after rigourous exercise by the children it rose to forty six degrees. Henry Morris the Education Secretary was now a frequent visitor, and the principle for Further Education discussed evening classes. Although this was not in fact the first village college, it provided the blueprint for those established later.

By 1924 the cookery, woodwork and laundry classes were held in a new annexe, but had to be suspended due to shortage of fuel. Two teachers and the head took thirty four children to the British Empire Exhibition at Wembley. That summer the school temperatures were between ninety and one hundred and ten degrees Fahrenheit in the sun, although the winter weather had been severe again, with frozen pipes etc., buses not running and some children walked from Swaffham and Reach. On July 8th 1929 a short service of thanksgiving was held for the recovery of His Majesty the King from his illness. In 1932 a class of thirty three occupied the Jubilee Reading room. Twenty new desks, sixty bibles and seventy two hymn books were delivered. In 1934 china bowls were fitted in the cloakrooms and electric lighting in all the classrooms. On May 3rd 1935 a short ceremony was held to commemorate the Silver Jubilee of His Majesty King George V. Each child was given a copy of John Buchan's 'The King's Grace' and on the 6th the school closed for the celebrations. The Ministry of Health condemned the water supply for drinking purposes in November. In 1938 a new greenhouse was completed, the work of glazing having been done by four boys without one pane of glass being broken, and the Unwin cup was awarded for the best kept school garden. As the second World War started evacuees were housed in a clubroom at the King William public house, the room being decorated by pupils. On 23rd June 1939 gas mask practices were held and in the July a pupil was sentenced at court for petty larceny to be birched and another put in care until he was eighteen.

My first teacher was Miss Eileen Halliday being in her class for two years, and for the following two I was taught by Miss Swann (the same person previously mentioned as the Sunday School Superintendent). Miss Bowyer took us for needlework and domestic science. Some foods were still rationed and I remember these included dried fruit, fats, and dried eggs. I thoroughly enjoyed my time here. School dinners were cooked by the some of the older girls and Miss Wolf, a teacher here for many years recalls the time when Miss Bowyer was sick and she was left in charge, her classroom being linked to the domestic science room by a hatch. At twelve o'clock when she opened the hatch to prepare to serve the dinners she discovered the girls standing around, the fire out and no dinner cooked. They knew how to do the cooking but not how to light the fire, nor, it seemed had the sense to tell her that it was out. On 9th April, 1946 there were celebrations of songs and dances with a public meeting in the evening to celebrate the schools centenary at which Mr Henry Morris was present. The school also functioned as a rest centre for the evacuees until they had been billeted.

In 1947 one hundred hot meals were taken to Swaffham Prior, Reach and St. Andrews School, Burwell, and another one hundred and twenty served on the premises. This year also saw the building of a new school canteen. The school leaving age was raised to fifteen and fourteen year olds came by bus from Fordham and Chippenham. On May 3rd 1948, eighteen boys stayed away from school and went to see Cambridge United play the Australians at Fenners in Cambridge, official permission having been refused. In 1949 the Methodist Sunday school was used as a classroom. In 1953 David Shepherd, later Anglican Bishop of Liverpool came to give a talk on the forthcoming M.C.C. tour of Australia as well as on Christian matters. A new hall/gymnasium was opened in 1958 on 23rd January but there were complaints of deficiencies in the design. In 1962 all school leavers were given Bibles by Gideon's International. 1965 saw the laying of the foundations of the present village college.

Plate 156. Jubilee Reading Room, 1990.   John Richardson

Plate 157. Double lock-up, 1990.   John Richardson

Plate 158. The Forge.

Plate 159. J. Lawrence, T. Lawrence and A. Flack firing a tyre outside the forge with the British School in the background, 1930s.

Plate.160. The Causeway showing the British School, in the 1920s.

Plate 161. Traction engine owned by Jaby Turner which was used at the coronation celebrations in 1911 on the recreation ground to boil water for making the tea.

Plate 162. Farm steam engine; inscription on the plaque reads, "Farmer engine". (G)

Plate 163. Ploughing match. (G)

135

Plate 164. Collection of tractors - Festival of Britain celebrations 1951.   (G)

Plate 165. Service from farm cart, Festival of Britain 1951.   (G)

Plate 166. 'Ladies Football team' in 1900.

Plate 167. Football team 1904 which played Macintosh's of Cambridge in April 1904 and won 3-0.　　　　Courtesy Miss Winnifred Peachey

Plate 168. Cricket team.

Plate 169. Hospital parade in North Street. Man with bicycle is Harry Peachey.
Courtesy Miss Winnifred Peachey

Plate 170. Hospital car, July 23rd 1911.

Plate 171. Peace celebrations in 1919.   Courtesy Miss Winnifred Peachey

139

Plate 172. 1842 tithe map of Low Town, Photographed by the author while it was in the possession of Jim Townsend.

Plate 173 Granny Shaw's shop on the left in North Street.
Courtesy Cambridge County Records Office

Plate 174. Mr Goldspink in the doorway of his butcher's shop in the 1920s. His assistant, Mr Beer is on the right. (G)

Plate 175. Mr Goldspink's shop and delivery van in the 1920s. (G)

Opposite the school is the Jubilee Reading room, so named because it commemorates Queen Victoria's Jubilee referred to earlier in the old church magazine. Erected in 1889, for the first six years its reading material was confined to newspapers, which may well have been outdated by the time they were put out for public use. In 1895, it was opened as a library and the first librarian, Mr Ernest Webb a school teacher was paid two shillings a week to give out books one evening a week. During the winter it was opened for two hours one afternoon a week. Mr Webb was also responsible for cataloguing the books. The caretaker, Mr John Chapman was paid eight shillings per month. The reading room was open from 10 a.m. to 10 p.m. and the fire would be lit at 4 p.m.

In 1896 books were hired from the Popular Book Club and this continued for a number of years. Vandalism broke out during this same year and the culprits were banned from the Reading Room for a month. Their names were read out at the Council meeting and they each received a warning letter. For some time there was a Registrar in attendance in the Reading Room at certain times each week. In 1910 when further trouble occurred a letter was written to the culprits' parents threatening legal action if there were any more complaints. This, together with the appearance of a letter in the Cambridge Independent Press seems to have solved the problem for the time being although the Reading Room was closed for a time after the First World War for similar reasons. During the Second World War the air raid siren was attached to this building. For the last twenty years or so the library has been housed at the village college.

Nearby stands the old lock-up, probably built in the early part of the nineteenth century, interesting because it was a double one, with separate doors. During the Second World War it housed the fire engine but now is used for storage. At the time of writing it seems the deeds cannot be found.

Adjacent to the lock up is the old forge which housed two furnaces. This building was built of clunch in 1710 although there had been a forge on this site since before 1600. Jim and Tom Lawrence were the last blacksmiths here and it was once the centre of village life. Children, including myself, have stood and watched as the horses were shod and ironwork beaten into shape. The metal rims of cart wheels were expanded by heating them with lighted turves and then slipping them onto the wooden wheels. The Lawrences closed the forge in 1953, but it was restored and brought back to life for a time in the early 1980s but it is now closed. The forge housed a huge pair of bellows made in 1851 and which once belonged to the late Mr Bill Sargent from Lode. The wages for pumping the bellows in the early 1900s would be a penny a day.

I remember the shop on the left just past the forge as a haberdashers which was run by two sisters, Misses C. and E. Dalzell from Exning. Number 107, built in the seventeenth century was until 1827 the White Hart Inn with a stable and coach house. A little further on I remember the 'Bushell Inn' with a row of cottages behind it, now all demolished and the land built upon. The road on the left is Hythe Lane leading to Hythe Bridge and the recreation ground. I don't know how long there has been a cricket team in Burwell but it was revived in 1890. During my teens I used to help Mrs Rene Gathercole with the cricket teas on a Saturday afternoon.

Opposite the site of the Bushell which was demolished in 1967, is the Fox Inn, the oldest part of which was built in the early seventeenth century. It was recorded as an ale house in 1764. On what is now the car park there was once a low building used in turn by a religious sect, then as storage for fruit and later as a fish and chip shop. The Fox in the past was the scene of many an auction and sale of land and property.

December 15th, 1848 saw the first meeting of the Burwell Agricultural Society. In the morning all was hustle and bustle, and by ten o'clock twenty lusty ploughmen and twenty good ploughs were in the field, an excellent one lent by Mr Ball for the occasion. It was the unanimous opinion of competent judges that the ploughing was first-rate. One part of the field was allotted to boys under eighteen to take part in a separate class for special prizes. Only men employed by Burwell farmers were allowed to enter and each ploughed half an acre. In the afternoon upwards of twenty gentlemen sat down to an excellent and substantial dinner at the Fox Inn: the magnificent presentation brought great credit to Mr Danby. Henry Johnson, Esq, presided, and throughout the day the greatest hilarity and harmony prevailed. On the removal of the cloth the chairman gave successfully 'The Queen', 'Prince Albert', and other loyal toasts. During the afternoon the successful competitors were called in and received their prizes from him. He addressed them appropriately, complimenting each on the manner of his work. They beamed with delight, and expressed deep gratitude to the society for its generosity. They were all regaled with a substantial dinner and spent a happy day. Prizes ranged from five to twenty shillings and the men were cautioned not to squander their winnings. Burwell is always proverbial for its hospitality to strangers who may be sure of finding a warm reception.

Plate 176. North Street.

Number 1 North street on the corner of Hythe Lane, often referred to as Hee Lane, housed Mrs Bridgeman's general store, where my mother did her shopping. The present shop is a new building. Number 4 opposite, was a butchers owned by Mr Goldspink. Later it became a fishmongers, then a butchers again before becoming a newsagent. Number 3 on the left, Brown's garage which is just past the present Co-op, was once a farmhouse, then a doctor's surgery but was once used by a chemist. Opposite was another farmhouse part of which was converted to a shoe shop after the death of the farmer. This is all now demolished and the land developed. Its timber frame and tie beams suggest that Oak Farm at number 12 is probably early seventeenth century. At one time, a hole some two feet above floor level gave access from one bedroom to another. Beside number 12 is Swan Alley, a narrow lane joining North Street with Silver Street.

Lower down on the left at number 29 is the Grange which was at one time a hairdressers run by the Clarkes, and where I had my first perm. One room was removed in order to straighten the street and during the war it provided a billet.

Plate 177. Primitive Methodist Chapel, 1990.   John Richardson

Opposite is another chapel, the Primitive Methodist, now used for storage. A report of 1863 states that 'the Primitive Methodists, commonly called Ranters, held a camp meeting in North Street on Sunday evening last. Like most meetings of this nature, we regret to learn that it ended in a sad scene of drunkeness and disorder'. I couldn't help wondering if the writer of this report had misconstrued the facts and these meetings were akin to the day of Pentecost as described in chapter two of the Book of Acts.

I understand from Mr Ernie Palmer who lives near the chapel and who, with his wife Gladys, used to play the organ, that camp meetings were held in a meadow behind the Grange. On Good Fridays Faith Teas were held, so named because it was through faith that each individual was able to provide sufficient food. The tea was made in the copper of a house nearby where on washdays the men's shirts were cleaned. Ernie's father organised concerts to raise money for the organ. Ernie was originally a wheelwright and in 1925 he sold complete farm carts for fourteen pounds and ten shillings each. Iron railings and an iron gate were removed from the front entrance during the First World War. The chapel closed in 1939 and in 1940 was sold for the modest sum of twenty seven pounds. Built in 1857 number 35, a private residence was the former 'Queen's Arms'.

Plate 178. Glory Alexander Evangelical meeting with banners.

Burwell House, now an educational establishment, was privately owned until about twenty six years ago, and one of my aunts was private secretary to Laurie Wallace, a Turf Accountant when he was the owner. The oldest part of the House dates back to 1787, the main staircase having been built in the early 1800s. It was the home of Ann and of Edward Ball, MP county magistrate, farmer and merchant. In 1858 it was bought by William Dunn and fifteen years later was taken over by George Townsend. By 1875 it was back in the Ball's family, occupied by Thomas, the coprolite and manure manufacturer.

I have been to many functions here including a Whist Drive which the choir organised when raising funds for the cassocks and surplices for the ladies choir. I also belonged to a group which used to meet in one of the upper rooms for play rehearsals.

Plate 179. Burwell House.

A bakery stood at Number 50, later becoming a butchers, then a bakers again before reverting to a private house. The date over the door of number 55 is 1706. This was once a corn chandlers before becoming an antique shop. Number 67 is the Anchor public house where a porch covers an ancient well discovered in 1979. It was fourteen feet deep and contained five feet of water.

It was here at the Anchor that the fifth anniversary of the Goshan Lodge of Peaceful brothers was held on 7th October 1850. Sixty members sat down to a fine dinner provided by Davey, their host. The afternoon and evening passed very pleasantly and after a good supper the company separated. Apparently the funds were not so plentiful as might have been wished.

A story which was reported in the Burwell Chronicles, which may well have taken place around here concerns Mrs Pool who lived in this area and was very anxious about the amount of money her husband was spending on drink. A friend in whom she confided suggested she put some money in the bank. After a while her husband

Plate 180. Barges under construction.

Plate 181. Horse drawn barge on an outing.

Plate 182. The staff of young girl employees with baskets and chairs in 1920 at E. Knott's basket making premises.

Plate 183. The bathing shed decorated for the regatta on August 1st 1910.

Plate 184. Swimming sports day, August 4th 1913.

Plate 185. The Maid's Head Public House.   Courtesy Cambridge Antiquarian Society

became suspicious and demanded to know where the money was going. Eventually she led him along to the river and showed him where she had hidden the money: in the *river* bank. He seized her and threw her in the river holding her under the water with a spade until she drowned.

For many years number 69 housed Roger Fullers the butchers. Behind numbers 69 and 71 was Burnt Yard, housing the barge building firm of Prentice Brothers which ceased production in 1920 but continued to carry out repairs until 1936. It was probably here or near here where one could board a pleasure boat and for the sum of sixpence enjoy a river trip from Burwell to Upware. On the north side of Burnt Yard was a maltings and the cut from the Lode (a reach of water) would bring horse drawn boats and barges bearing cargoes of grain and coal to the maltings. The maltings was later converted to five or six cottages, and in Jerusalem Yard there was a group of cottages and a pond. Even though the water through which the horses would trot was green and stagnant it is purported to have made the best home brewed beer in Burwell.

Jerusalem Yard was so named because it was once thought to have been a Jewish burial ground. A similar ground is thought to have existed in Mill Lane and was probably used by the Jewish families at Exning. At number 75 was Bert Knott's basket works. Bert, a cripple, started his business at number 107. He employed about a dozen young women and youths. The products included measures of a half and one bushel for fruit for market, buckets with handles for fruit picking, clothes' baskets, bicycle baskets and high backed chairs, some of which were highly decorated. The business was started in 1913 but closed in 1926, probably because of the slump period of 1926/7. Osiers were grown at Reach, Upware and Burwell. These willows were grown especially for basket making and were planted on each side of the river or where the land was likely to flood. Within three years when they were anything up to nine feet in length they would be cut, soaked and peeled by drawing them between two pieces of iron and then soaked in water to make them pliable. Later Bert Knott's original shop became a fish and chip shop which closed after a fire and became a clothing shop, and is now run by a market gardener. Sedge growing was another similar industry. It was cut and used for building walls, thatching roofs, making baskets, horse collars, and even coarse clothing for rough work.

Plate 186. Stacking Peat.

Plate 187. Peat fen.

Plate 188. Digging peat in 1905.

Plate 189. Mrs Durrant loading peat turves. Her husband sold turves in North Street.

Plate 191. Pump in North Street.

Plate 190. Alex Hobb's shop.

Plate 192. Pump in North Street, 1904.

Plate 193. Evelyn Durrant with his horses.   (G)

Plate 194. Baptist Chapel, 1905.

Plate 195. Baptist Chapel.

Plate 196. Re-opening of the Baptist Chapel in 1968.

Plate 197. Baptist Sunday School in 1930.

Plate 198. Baptism in the river.

Plate 199. North Street. Courtesy Mrs F. Horton

The present Lode from which the cut at Burnt Yard runs was probably cut in the mid seventeenth century and appears on a map of the fen of 1695. T.T. Balls chemical works had its own transport of three steam tugs and gangs of lighters. At the rear of number 79 a large barn has been converted to a beautiful house, one of several conversions in the village.

Number 81 North Street, until quite recently known as the Black Bat was built in the seventeenth century and enlarged in 1770. A three foot deep cellar which was used as a dairy, suggests that it had probably been a farmhouse. In the 1870s a shop was opened by Mr G.F. Lepla who came from Corfe Castle in Dorset. Second hand double front windows which came from Muncies, the Jewellers in Cambridge were installed. When the LePlas family went bankrupt in 1894 the shop had to close. It was reopened in 1897 by Mr and Mrs Hobbs whose son Alex continued to run it until it was sold in 1965. When horses became scarce during the First World War he delivered goods from the wicker side-car of his motorcycle. After the war he owned a larger motorcycle for which he built a large box. In 1962 however, he bought a van. His uncle had begun the delivery in the days of horse-drawn vans, travelling to the Swaffhams, Bottisham, Lode and Reach. I well remember Alex, his wife and his son, David coming up to the Guildhall to the Badminton club, where David would try out his latest magic trick. It was in 1929 that Alex put a knocker in the shape of a bat on the side door of the house which gave it the name of the Black Bat, when in 1977 it was opened for a while as a restaurant.

A cinder track along the river bank over a footbridge and across the weirs from number 89, formerly the Rose public house once led to a galvanised iron shed. This had been built at a cost of sixteen pounds as a changing room for a swimming club. The club held its first sports day on August Bank holiday 1908. People came from as far away as Soham and Newmarket and in later years the crowds numbered nearly two thousand. Children were taught to swim here during school time by Mr Harold Fuller. He would stand on the diving board with a nine foot pole which had a rope attached to it holding learners by the chest with a belt at the other end of it. The learner would be taken backwards and forwards in a semi circle from the steps to the bank doing the breast stroke. In June 1908, the swimmers found themselves covered in tar. A tin of tar was recovered from the river which was thought to have been placed there by people who objected to seeing others in bathing costumes, despite the fact that these reached to the knees. A young boy who learnt to swim here rescued a small boy from drowning and was recommended for a medal from the Life Saving Society. On one occasion the organising committee obtained some racing eights from Cambridge and bump races were held between the bathing shed and the Cock up Bridge. During the winter 1913-14 some tough lads decided to have a dip every morning about 7 o'clock often having to break the ice. They changed by the light of a candle while Beatrice oil stoves heated the Lode water for an after dip cup of tea. With the outbreak of the First World War club membership dwindled and efforts to revive it failed, although swimming continued for some years until the shed was removed. Subsequently, a popular spot for swimming was near the manure works and this is where I had my first taste of bathing in the river. I wore a ruched bathing costume and when I had finished my bathe and came out to change I discovered that I was carrying half the mud of the river with me inside the bathing costume.

Another cut existed between numbers 77 and 79 and another between 85 and 89. It was in the cut between 77 and 79 where the baptismal services were held. Numbers 92 and 96 were originally almshouses and number 101, now Thatchers was formerly the Maid's Head.

Many of the houses, particularly in North Street had open hearths and for the poor at least, turf or peat as it is more usually known provided a cheap and widely available source of fuel.

About three hundred and fifty years ago the Old Fen or Poor Fen of one hundred and ninety acres, was left for the exclusive benefit of the poor of Burwell. It seems that many years ago the deeds and other documents relating to this were destroyed or lost. Between three and four hundred pounds a year was raised from peat. This supplied fuel for a whole year and any surplus was sold to their more prosperous neighbours and the money divided equally according to the labour each poor man had contributed.

In earlier times the 'sods' or 'hassocks' had been dug with a heart-shaped spade but by about 1856 a tool eighteen inches long and four inches wide with an iron flange, called a becket, was used. This enabled the work to be done systematically and the sods lined up in rows to dry. (The public house, the Spade and Becket in Cambridge owes its name to this practice). Peat was formed from the hypnum moss and the smoke from it made the eyes water. As the land was drained so less moss grew, but at one time it grew about four inches in twelve years and would have been dug in rotation. When it was dug it was composed of ninety per cent water and by the time the spring sunshine and wind had completed the drying out process, the block would have shrunk to about the size of a building brick. Barges would have taken some of the turves to Cambridge, near Barnwell Bridge where they were used for firing bricks. Year after year Poor Fen became more involved in tax payments and a part of the land was put up for auction for the arrears. Rev. Baines was persuaded to attend the sale and buy the land. He did so and was repaid by parish officers who paid the tax of nine pounds per year. Some objected but as it prevented the poor from being a drain on the parish it was judged worth the expense. Prior to this in the 1840-50s a Cambridge solicitor came into possession of an estate adjoining this fen. He took a great interest in the welfare of the poor and befriended them. He decided that the land would be more profitable if it were cultivated and divided up into allotments and let to the poor, and a sum of two thousand pounds was borrowed on mortgage to prepare the land for cultivation. But the majority of 'Burwellites' objected and a petition of one thousand signatures was drawn up. With only two thousand people in the village and only those over fourteen allowed to sign this was a sizable number. Only six of those eligible refused. An Ely surveyor coming to prepare the land was met by hundreds of Burwell people who diverted his attention by directing him either to the ditch or the road. Sensibly, he chose the road. He then procured some labourers from Ely while watching from a safe distance. But the Ely men having heard the full story from the Burwell men declined to oblige him. Several efforts were made to divide up the land. Twelve policemen arrived from London to be confronted by several hundred Burwell men, insistent that the land was theirs and while they would not allow trespassers they did not wish to cause a disturbance.

    They had dug a wide ditch to prevent further trespasses when the attendance of a county magistrate, a Captain Alexander Cotton was sought. As he reached North Street he saw hundreds of labourers hurrying to Poor fen. He saluted one and asked him where he was going with his shovel. 'To my work', came the reply. The Captain immediately asked the man to give up his shovel. The man replied, 'it is my shovel and I'll not part with it'. The twelve policemen approached where upon the villagers closed ranks round their friend. The Captain proceeded to Old Fen where stood a formidable array of four hundred sturdy peasants armed with bludgeons, spades and other menacing weapons. The Riot Act was produced and read but could not be heard as the villagers set up a yell. The magistrate did not acquire possession and he and his men sounded a retreat. A regiment of cavalry soldiers and a body of infantry were then despatched to Burwell. The approaching visit became known throughout the neighbourhood and hundreds of people poured into Burwell. There were forty vehicles at one inn and all the public houses were crowded. Sympathy for the poor ran so deep that neighbouring places pledged support and in Newmarket in one day alone forty pounds was raised. Fordham, Soham, Reach and the Swaffhams all offered to subscribe. Sadly, at an early hour the cry was raised that the soldiers were on Poor fen. Deviously they had marched from Soham across Wicken and unseen by anyone had taken possession of the land. Sixty Hussars under the command of Captain Peel and headed by Rev. Mr Bennett one of the County magistrates moved to the scene of action but turned back after marching a quarter of a mile up the Fen Drove to retrace their steps to Bury via Newmarket, the quagmires and deep pits being too much for the horses.

A double line of soldiers was drawn up on Poor Fen and although there was a great number of people there was no disturbance. Some of the ringleaders who had formerly clashed with the police were rounded up and taken by soldiers to the Fox Inn. The land was claimed. After an hour and a half's marching twelve soldiers were left and about forty navies sworn in as special constables and then set to work levelling the land. Crowds followed the prisoners and soldiers to the Fox. Some of the men were discharged but six were handcuffed and taken to Cambridge by omnibus. The village was soon cleared and about forty soldiers were left to keep guard. Another account of Burwell's riots blames the people from High town for taking the turves from the Low Town people causing a fight which had to be quelled by the militia.

Due to the increasing mortgage on the land in 1964, by permission of the Charity Commissioners an auction took place in the Gardiner Memorial Hall. Sufficient money was raised in order to pay off the mortgage and the capital invested. This realises about two thousand four hundred pounds annually which is used for heating or cash payments to about three hundred and fifty elderly people in

Burwell each year. Turves were still being sold at Reach in 1939 but turf cutting was banned then. The land which was formerly held in trust, is now cultivated.

Plate 200. Fen windmill, 1900.

Near the corner of Toyse Lane stands the Baptist Church. The first known Baptist in Burwell was a James Fuller who in 1790 left the Independent Church, became baptised and for ten years attended the Baptist Church at Soham alone. Three others were then baptised and the four continued to worship at Soham. When the Soham pastor changed his views to that of the Socinians they left. Socinians followed the doctrine of the Italian theologian Socinius (Lelio Sozzini 1525-62) and his nephew Fausto Sozzini (1539-1604) who denied the doctrine of the Trinity and the divinity of Christ. A Mrs Kempton formed the first Baptist School in 1815 and the rite of baptism of four people in the Name of the Sacred Three was administered the following year for the first time. After a time they began meeting in a house where the church flourished and several were baptised.

After joining with the Soham membership the group met together in a house near the present church. The owner of the house however, a Mr Shelverton, was opposed to dissenters and he expelled the tenant who was one of the members. Shelverton died, his family circumstances were reduced and the family died out.

During a thunderstorm in August 1835 the building was struck by lightning but the only stone to have shifted was one inscribed with the name of Shelverton. The next year a fire destroyed both this building and buildings nearby and it was left in ruins for some time. The ruins and nearby land were purchased by Mr William Pratt who laid the foundation stone for the chapel.

A substantial chapel was built using stones from the house and burnt-out buildings and also from a burial ground. Unfortunately Mr Pratt was a sick man and died in 1849 without being able to worship here. That same year a religious celebration took place when members of the chapel held their annual tea drinking celebrations. On the following day the town was decorated and the Sunday School children dressed in their best were regaled with tea and cake.

Two side galleries were opened in 1847 and the school room in 1882. An organ from a London church was installed in 1849 and 1931 saw the introduction of electric light. During the time in which it was united with Soham, twenty five people were dismissed and the church of Burwell was formed on 7th January, 1851, William C. Ellis becoming its first Pastor. The Ladies' Guild was formed in July, 1926 and the Young Peoples' Fellowship in September 1931. Other groups and clubs have been added in later years and I believe this is a flourishing, self-supporting church. In 1951 it celebrated its centenary with a reunion of past and present members of church and Sunday School, presidents of various bodies and ministers from other churches. This was presided over by the Moderator of the Cambridgeshire Baptist Association and the morning and evening services were conducted by Rev. Gilvert Laws D.D. of Norwich. Musical items were performed by the Young Peoples' Fellowship. Baptisms took place in the river until about 1905 when the chapel acquired a Baptistry.

Plate 201. The 'New' Mill in 1931.   Courtesy Cambridge Antiquarian Society

Plate 202. Old corn mill.

Further to the right is the turning to Toyse Lane along which at number 30 Mr Robert Wilson Howard had his dental surgery from 1926-1947. He also held a weekly surgery in Lakenheath often cycling there for the purpose. When he retired he bred pedigree goats achieving great success in milking records. His pedigree dogs were prize winners at shows. A Miss Wilson ran the Welcome Mission in two converted bungalows. Old ladies became residents and there was a small chapel for worship.

Back in North Street a little way past the turning to Toyse Lane is the old St. Andrew's Mission Church. The Foundation stone for this Mission church as it was called, was laid in 1863 by Miss Hughes, sister of the curate.

Services had been held in the Anchor which according to the report was quite unfitting.

A house was also built for the school mistress. The church opened its doors on 12th November, 1863, when four hundred people and a number of clergy attended morning service, the collection amounting to sixteen pounds, thirteen shillings and ninepence farthing. The Archdeacon preached from John 4:10 and after lunch at the Anchor Inn six hundred people attended a service in the afternoon when a forceful sermon was preached from 1 Corinthians by Rev. W. Emery, while Rev. W. Plows of Kentford played the harmonium. The collection after this amounted to fourteen pounds, thirteen shillings and fivepence. A parochial tea was served in Mr W. Bridgeman's barn which had been decorated for the occasion with flags, evergreen, corn and mottoes. More addresses followed in which it was stressed that it was the duty of the laity to make sure that every Christian man prepared himself for the other world. This was to be a free church where rich and poor met together. At first it also served as the school. On St. Andrew's Day, 30th November, 1871, the school which had cost four hundred and fifty pounds to build was opened and the church rededicated. Local children between the age of three and fourteen years were admitted but later when they were eleven they went on to Grammar Schools or to the Burwell Secondary Modern School. The school was big enough until the infants' room was needed as a canteen for mid-day meals, when the infant class moved into the church. Each day the school began and ended with corporate worship. The school ceased to be used in 1961 when the new primary school was built in Ness Road.

Plate 203. St. Andrew's Church taken just before it closed, 1990.
John G. Richardson

Plate 204. Interior of St. Andrew's Church. Courtesy Mrs F. Horton

Plate 205. St. Andrew's school, 1905, back row: Miss Ball, Charlie Hawes, Ernie Hawes, - Harding, Florrie Hawes, Annie Redhead; next row: - Simmons, Maggie Harding, Eddie Hawes, Winnie Hawes, Bert Hawes, L. Matthews, Vic Barton, - Mathews, - Barton, ?; next row: Olive Simmons, Jessie Clack, Dot Hobbs, Rose Hobbs, Alice Redhead, Gladys Hawes, Bertha Redhead, Dot Mathews, - Mathews, V. Simmons; front row: Stephen Harding, - Harding, - Harding.

Plate 206. Burwell Band in the 1920s.

Plate 207. Burwell Band after winning the Sir Thomas Challenge cup with 85 points. Back row left to right: W. Brown (Newmarket), B. Clarke, A. Hawes, W. Casburn, C. Stewart (Headmaster at Newmarket); middle row: W. Barton, F. Jennings, G. Turner, Joan Hawes, W. Mitchell, R. Hobbs, E. Woodruffe (Newmarket); front row: J. Fuller, R. Bentley, Len Golding (Conductor), Laurie Wallis (President), F. Peachey, R. Turner, H. Smith. (G)

Sadly, this little church has had to close as it would have cost thousands of pounds to repair, although up to the time of its closure twice monthly early morning services were held. The last service to be held there was on Sunday, 12th February, 1990 when the Arch Deacon, the Ven David Walser preached the sermon. The service was candlelit as the electric wiring was not thought to be safe. I was one of four of the original female members of the St. Mary's choir to be in the congregation that day and I recognised one of the male members of that choir. Regrettably, permission has been granted for the building to be put to commercial use.

I have referred to the Burwell band several times as it played for various social occasions but it was disbanded during the First World War. During the mid 1920s it was revived and became known as the Burwell Excelsior Band rehearsing twice weekly in St. Andrew's school, collecting instruments from homes in the village.

Money was raised for uniforms and the band made regular appearances as it had in the past, at fêtes, hospital Sunday parades and other functions in Burwell and the surrounding villages. Later, new green uniforms were purchased and the band has flourished through the years, now rehearsing at the Fox. After the Second World War, under the baton of Mr L. Golden, a retired Royal Marine's bandsman, it won several contests, including the Sir Thomas Challenge cup in the East Anglian Brass Band Association, with eighty five points, beating Hilgay by two points. It was then agreed that the band should be run as an evening class at the Secondary Modern School, a conductor being supplied by the Education Authority. As time wore on it became difficult to retain a conductor and by 1973 the band had only twelve members and so it was decided to make it an affiliated member of the college classes, finding its own conductor. For the next fifteen years, under the baton of Mr Dennis Gilbey numbers increased to thirty and new uniforms were purchased. However, once again the numbers decreased and in order to survive in 1988, it was decided to hold evening classes to provide instruction and practice.

Plate 208. North Street showing Briarwood on the left, about 1910. Courtesy Mrs Olive Johnson

Plate 209. The Sabberton family in about 1910, back row left to right: Vivienne, Teddy, Olive; front row: Mrs Sabberton, Eileen, Mr Sabberton.   Courtesy Mrs Olive Johnson

'Briarwood', or number 105 North Street was once the home of a Newmarket butcher by the name of Sabberton. He had his slaughterhouse here and when sheep arrived at Fordham Railway Station he fetched them and walked them back to Briarwood. He had five daughters and two sons but unfortunately one daughter died here at the age of twelve while under anaesthetic to have her tonsils removed. One of the other daughters, Olive married my father's brother and two others still live in the village. One, Miss Eileen Sabberton still lives in North Street and is well known in the village for all the work she does in raising money for cancer research. During the Second World War the army occupied the premises after which they became a carton making factory until they were bought by Tillotsons. Number 115 was for many years used as a shop selling confectionery, tobacco and provisions which were taken round on a two-wheeled covered cart or bicycle. I wonder if the driver was Mrs Sophie Millar. She sold vegetables and so on from a hand-cart, walnuts costing one penny a hundred. Another character, Frank Feakes followed horses with a wheelbarrow, broom and shovel. My guess is that he would not have been the only one to do so. A Maurice Hatley lived in a caravan in North street. With a 'tail-coat and a floppy hat' he rode a bicycle scratching a precarious living from pruning trees.

Plate 210. Sabberton's pony and trap: Mr Sabberton, Teddy and Olive.
Courtesy Mrs Olive Johnson

Many other notable people have traversed the streets of Burwell including Mr William Heffer, who was brought up in Burwell and later founded Heffer's Bookshop in Cambridge.

Dyson's Drove is a short road leading from North Street to the bridge over the weirs where it becomes Little Fen Drove. Richard the brother of T.T. Ball, started the brick making industry in 1850. By 1864 it was operating beside the chemical artificial manure works. The clay was dug in the summer and allowed to weather in winter. It was then put into boxes for drying and firing. The men would wear moleskin gloves to eliminate finger prints on the bricks. By 1933, with changes in the processes of production a large kiln capable of holding over four hundred thousand bricks was constructed which produced the famous 'Burwell Whites'. One contract was for underground offices in Whitehall, London, used by Sir Winston Churchill. At this time sixty men were employed here. In the early 1930s Fisons took over the company and in 1966 it was bought out by Ibstock Brick and Tile Co. but like the Coprolite and chemical manure manufacturers before it, it ceased to function in August 1971 by which time the average wages of the men was about twenty pounds per week. In March 1972 the two one hundred and eighty foot high chimneys were demolished by explosives to produce ten thousand tons of rubble.

Plate 211. North Street, 1900.

On the left of Priory Farm was the old Cock-up or draw bridge others being at the Anchor yard and at the junction of Burwell and Wicken Lodes. Near Harrison's Drove and not far from there right in the depths of the fens once lived old Tom Harrison, the last of the real Fen punt-gunners in this area. He lived in a hut made of black turf blocks two foot thick, rivetted with withies and plastered outside with stiff clay to make it waterproof. Legend has it that it was no higher than a man inside, with one or two small windows and a hole in the roof to allow the smoke to escape. Old Tom rarely took off his clothes and never washed unless he fell in the dyke. His gunning punt was clinker built and about sixteen feet long. He lived the life of a hermit with a long-legged curly coated mongrel, half retriever and half spaniel. He was racked with ague and in summer he gathered 'paigles' in the fen meadows and made 'paigle tea' or cowslip wine. When he sold his ducks and geese, eels and tench he was partly paid in laudanum - the foundation of the 'ager mixture' which doped his shivering limbs and kept the ague at bay for a few hours. Another cure for 'ague' was a tea made from the poppyheads of the white poppies which were grown in most of the gardens, and this was also given to soothe teething children. This opium mixture was also given by the fen women to prevent their babies demanding attention while they slaved on the land. By 1860 when drainage was well established the 'ague' was less prevalent.

Plate 212. Boot repairer.

Successful drainage of the Fens was carried out by the Earl of Bedford in the seventeenth century with assistance from some Dutch engineers. This left behind a large area of black soil. The Earl formed the Company of Gentlemen Adventurers. At a time when their wages were only twelve to fifteen shillings a week their leather thigh boots would cost fen workers three pounds per pair. These 'tool men' dug fen drainage dykes by hand.

Plate 213. Demolishing St. Andrew's School.   Courtesy Jim Neale

Farmers also kept bees and made mulled mead from the honey, a drink which appealed to visitors. Norman's Mill, was one of a number of mills that used to don the landscape, some being used for drainage. It is probably Norman's Mill which was taken to Wicken Fen.

The concrete droves into the fens were made during the Second World War. In the mid 1800s these droves were forty foot wide tracks and ran straight for four to five miles. When the land was being drained the wheels of the farmers' carts had tyres of between six and eight inches wide. But it was easier to travel on horseback. The ruts which carriage wheels made could be as much as twelve to eighteen inches deep in the black peat. If the worst happened and horse and trap toppled into a drain several men pulling ropes were needed to recover them.

It was the custom for fen parishes to appoint yearly two men to the Saxon office of reeves to superintend and manage the droves and roads. In 1942 a barge took the King and Queen up Burwell Lode to see the land reclamation scheme.

Plate 214. Artificial manure works in 1932.
Courtesy Cambridge Antiquarian Society

Following Tom Harrison in Burwell Fen was the Badcock family who thought nothing of a 'mess o' water-rats' for supper. Father Badcock drank 'poppyhead tea' to ward off the ague and in summer made 'paigle tea' and distilled potato wine, raw and potent. He was a good man, who worked hard and made the six-mile trudge to chapel each Sunday. Burwell housed a tough race of Fen Tigers and others included Ted Jarvis, 'Cacker' Casburn the unctous Bible-banger and 'Fenner Bob'. The Crawleys, who lived by the side of the Casburns were a lawless lot and were mixed up with a secret gang of sheep-stealers and farm-robbers, who terrorised the district for years until they were rounded up by Police-Sergeant Plant. The gang had their headquarters at Pout Hall an old thatched picturesque house with six rooms which stood at the junction of Reach and Burwell Lodes. It had been built to serve as an inn by John Peachey in the mid nineteenth century but the licence for the sale of alcohol could never be obtained, so the sheep stealers took it over. It also provided a rendezvous for illicit beer-selling and other illegal activities. The gang brewed their own beer and went on forays at night to lonely farms. Sheep were rounded up, skinned, cut up, and taken by boat to a wharf belonging to the last house in North Street, an old building built in the seventeenth century by one of the Dutch drainers, and which had an underground room. At harvest time the gang would steal boatloads of corn, thrashed out with wooden flails on a sail-cloth, bag it up and take it to the underground granary in the old house. These utterly lawless raiders ventured far afield and so desperate were they that they held many of the outlying inhabitants of farms and cottages in terror of their lives. Finally, Police-Sergeant Plant, with a constable or two, surprised the gang one night with their booty. When they resisted arrest he went for them, broke one man's arm with his truncheon, left several others stunned and bleeding and captured the ring-leaders, although some slipped his net.

Plate 215. Boys diving off the cock-up bridge in the 1930s. (G)

The name of Pout Hall was probably derived from the name of an eel which abounded in the waters near here. The eel-pout is about eight to twelve inches long and weighs two to three pounds. A long wicker-work basket, i.e. trap or grig, meaning eel, was used to trap the eels. It would be filled with live worms and when the eels entered to feed they would be trapped by a one way valve. Near Pout Hall have been found two Roman slave chains with a lock and in the same area the whole skeleton of a whale. A tazza with talc beads, probably the treasures of an Asiatic soldier of the Roman foreign Legion and coins from the late Bronze-age have also been found. In other areas of the fen, skeletons have been found of a whale, a bear and the bones of a pelican. Fishing in the lode has been known to produce crayfish, perch, roach, bream, tench and eels. Animals found in these fens include the martin, polecat, black rat, viper, otter and the black adder which was quite dangerous. Rumour has it that the polecat is making a comeback unless of course it never really disappeared altogether. Birds which have been spotted here have included the bustard, bitten, dotterel, goshawk, ruff, buzzard, hawk, white owl, brown owl, linnet, quail, partridge, pheasant, snipe, curlew, lapwing and the nightingale.

Plate 216. Burwell Lode.

Dr Charles Lucas' father who came to Burwell in 1835 bought seven acres of land in 1856 near Toft Farm in High Town Drove which at that time was under water and despite the most strenuous efforts being made in 1852, two thousand acres were still flooded. It turned out to be one of the richest coprolite lands in Burwell.

Plate 217. The brickworks. (G)

Plate 218. Mr Albert Gathercole presenting cups to the retired at the brickworks. (G)

Plate 219. The brickworks showing the railway. (G)

The industry began in 1858, the men earning good wages, of two to three pounds per week. The farmers complained of a shortage of labour, as an agricultural worker would only be earning about ten shillings per week. Coprolite was thought originally to come from the dung of prehistoric animals but most was formed from shells, the land having been originally covered by shallow seas teeming with fish and shell fish. The word coprolite originated from a Greek word meaning dung stone. The coprolites were recovered by digging a trench about three feet wide where the coprolite was found twelve to twenty feet below the surface and as the nodules were exposed and dug out the trench would be filled with the earth dug from the next trench. Three hundred tons could be obtained from one acre. After the loose soil had been washed from the fossils, they were ground, mixed with sulphuric acid, producing a cake which floated to the top, was taken off, dried and crushed to powder for application to the land. It is thought that some of the first superphosphates produced in Burwell were ground at the windmill in Newmarket Road. The necessity of a plentiful supply of sulphuric acid gave rise to a further industry when in the late 1800s a partnership was formed between Mr G.H. Colchester with Mr T.T. Ball founder of the business, a London expert who came to Burwell to organise and run the sulphuric acid plant. It began at a house, probably the Poplars in Low Road, but as it expanded the works were probably built on the lode in 1864, as this was the date on the chimney. Materials were imported from Spain, North Africa and North America. In about 1904 three and a half miles of standard gauge railway track was installed which linked up with the old G.E.R. line between Fordham and Soham now removed. The Lode also had a ferry on a chain which brought workmen from Reach to the chemical works.

Plate 220. Drainage mill on Hallard's Farm which was removed by 1931. Courtesy Cambridge Antiquarian Society

181

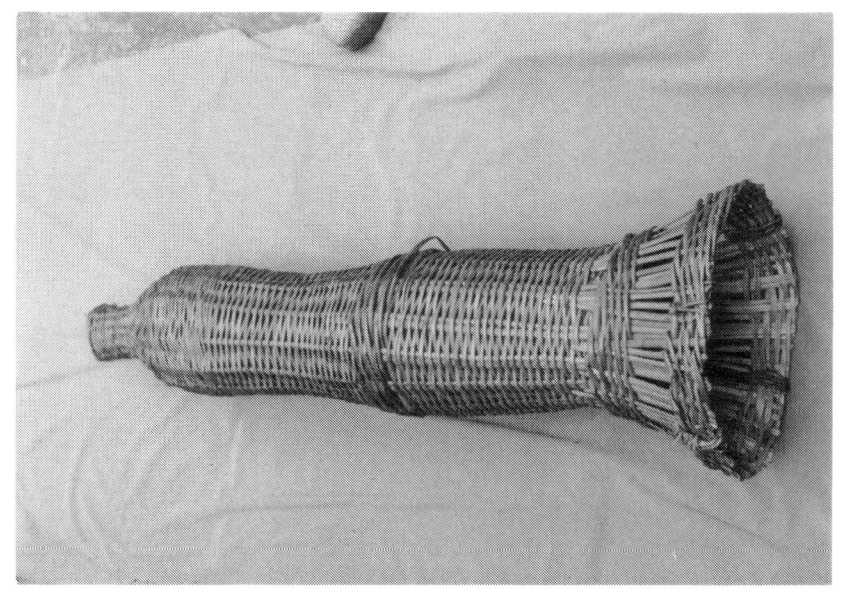

Plate 221. Eel trap.   Courtesy Cambridge Folk Museum

Plate 222. Mr Dunnett with his model yacht.

Plate 223. Bus terminus in North Street.

Plate 224. Judy's hole and squatters cottages.

Plate 225. Mary Jarvis at her cottage.

119, North Street was probably built around the mid 1500s. Later a granary, hay loft and dairy were added besides an upper floor. While the house was being altered both a scrap of paper with details of a hearth tax in 1600 and an ancient leather shoe were found. At one time the front parlour had been used as a draper's store and before that it was yet another public house, 'the Stag'. Laterly, it was known as Fred Peachey's Old House, his family having lived and farmed here for over one hundred and twenty years.

'Adventurer s' at 124 is another old cottage, originally two or three but now completely renovated and made into one. It is a grade II listed building of considerable architectural and historical merit.

At the end of North Street off the road on the left is Goose Hall Farm once occupied years ago by a man who kept a large number of geese and ducks which fed on the common grass and probably gave it its name.

A little way to the south of the farm stood a row of six thatched cottages built by 'squatters' and inhabited by typical fenmen who were rather tall and big, with very black hair, rough in their manners, cunning, independent and lawless. They lived chiefly by fishing and fowling and in summer helped with the harvest, turf digging and sedge cutting.

One of the customs of these fenmen was to put grass in their boots instead of wearing socks, this apparently kept the feet cool.

In the most northerly one an old woman lived alone, named Judy Finch. A description of Judy is given in the following doggerel.

> A wicked old crone,
> Who lived all alone,
> In a hut beside of the reeds,
> With a high-crowned hat
> And a black tom-cat,
> Whose looks were as bad as her deeds.

She had a very bad character and a vile reputation for dark deeds in matters of maternity affairs. If there were any devilry going on in the parish Judy Finch would surely be behind it. She was known as the 'wise woman' of the district but in earlier times would have been considered an 'old witch'. In 1843 she owned a pit near the road covering an area of one and a half acres and excavated to repair the lode banks. This was known as Judy's Hole. Years ago it was an ideal spot for skating and sliding in winter, being only about two feet deep, and therefore safe.

Now the hole has been filled in. Mrs Jarvis, an old lady of completely opposite character lived at the other end of the squatters' cottages. She was described as a Burwell Victorian Village Nurse and Parish Referee; noted for her good works and full of kindliness. She was of a cheerful disposition, scrupulously clean both in her person and in her home, thrifty, clever and at the beck and call of anyone in distress. She used both wild and garden plants for her cures, and salves of ground ivy, and plasters of white lily petals. Her garden was full of herbs and her cupboards full of physic and 'rubbing stuffs,' which she willing gave and administered with comfort and sympathy. She kept a few hens so as 'to have an egg by her', which she was always willing to give to sick friends. She lent a hand in maternity cases and was ready to help in all illnesses. She was a Wesleyan and went to church on Christmas Day, Good Friday and at Whitsun.

In his book, Dr Lucas recalls a few stories which I thought were worth relating. One concerned fen bread which was slate in colour. A few years after partaking of such bread at an inn, he had to attend a maternity case where twins had been born and granny took them down to the parlour to keep them warm by the fire. When the nurse later looked for them they were nowhere to be seen. Granny had put them on the dough which was rising in front of the fire. Later, after the dough had been baked the nurse noticed two loaves standing by themselves. Granny explained that she 'could not wash the dough where the babies were laid so I made it up into two loaves. They will do for father to eat; he won't mind'.

At a big house a little way into the fen occupied by a farmer of considerable means the maid serveant asked her mistress what meat they were to have for the kitchen dinner. 'Gal, give me a knife', said the mistress and taking it she went into the farmyard and cut off the tail of a dirty old pig and, throwing it on the table, said: 'Make that into a dumpling, that's the meat of the kitch' dinner'.

Another wealthy fen farmer had a protracted illness. One evening a friend called to see his wife, who was blunt, rough and outspoken. She said, 'I am worred to death, what with the *Soul Savers* (parsons), the *Devil Dodgers* (lawyers) and the *Body Snatchers* (doctors) I don't know how to carry on'.

Another story concerned an old bailiff who used to drive about in a cart because his feet were bad. He gave Dr Lucas two old match-boxes because 'I know you are fond of curiosities. There are two of my toe-nails which come off t'other day'. He added that, 'my feet have not touched water for the ten year. If I used that I should have the ager. When I do have the ager, I fix round my wrist an ounce of shag and I soon get cured'. Incidentally, 'the toe nails were twisted about like ram's horns and must have been of several years' growth'.

This brings us to the end of North Street, the road eventually leading to the Broads, where bronze battle-axes, daggers and other artefacts have often been found. It is probable that there was a bronze-age settlement in this neighbourhood.

And so we have seen a glimpse of the heritage and history of Burwell. To bring it up to the present times would fill another book at least.

At a recent Burwell at Large weekend held at the village college on 17th and 18th February 1990, over a thousand visitors came to view what Burwell had to offer and over sixty different groups and societies were represented. The bi-monthly community magazine of 'Clunch' first issued on January 3rd, 1976 keeps everyone well informed of all that is happening in Burwell today.

Suggested further reading

Ball, T.T., Account of Burwell Boy's School, Jubilee 1896
Ball, T.T., Life of James Smith (Baptist Minister) 1897
Burwell Chronicles, Cambridgeshire Collection: City Library
Burwell House, pamphlet
Cambridge Archives, County Records, Shire Hall
Cambridgeshire Collection, City Library
Cambridge Chronicles, Cambridgeshire Collection, City Library
Cambridge Evening News
Clunch: 1976-90 Burwell's Community Magazine
Ennion, E.A.R., Adventurer's Fen, 1949
Gathercole, A.F., Burwell and its Church, 1975
Gibbons, T., Burwell Fire, 1769
Goodridge, E., Burwell Methodist Church 150 years
Hutchin, B.D., Burwell Library 1850-1965, pub. 1972
Lethbridge, T.C., Anglo-Saxon Cemetery 1925.
Lethbridge T.C., Excavations at Burwell Castle, 1935
Lewis, J., Scratch Sun-Dial at Burwell St. Mary's Church
Lucas, Charles, Cambridge Standard, Burwell Fen Riots, 1935.
Lucas, Charles, Notes on the Old Guildhall
Lucas, Charles, The Fenman's World, 1930
Neale, Jim, Burwell & District Motor Service, Illustrated History
Newmarket Journal
Sayer, Walpole, A.G., A lecture on Burwell Church
Sayer, Walpole, A.G., History of St. Mary's Church
Sayer, Walpole, A.G., Notes on Burwell Church
Watts, G.W., Jim's Last Run, 1979
Wentworth-Day, J. History of the Fens